MALAYA'S FIRST YEAR AT THE UNITED NATIONS

The **Institute of Southeast Asian Studies (ISEAS)** was established as an autonomous organization in 1968. It is a regional centre dedicated to the study of socio-political, security and economic trends and developments in Southeast Asia and its wider geostrategic and economic environment. The Institute's research programmes are the Regional Economic Studies (RES, including ASEAN and APEC), Regional Strategic and Political Studies (RSPS), and Regional Social and Cultural Studies (RSCS).

ISEAS Publishing, an established academic press, has issued almost 2,000 books and journals. It is the largest scholarly publisher of research about Southeast Asia from within the region. ISEAS Publishing works with many other academic and trade publishers and distributors to disseminate important research and analyses from and about Southeast Asia to the rest of the world.

MALAYA'S FIRST YEAR AT THE UNITED NATIONS

As Reflected in Dr Ismail's Reports Home to Tunku Abdul Rahman

Compiled by

Tawfik Ismail & Ooi Kee Beng

ISEAS

Institute of Southeast Asian Studies
Singapore

First published in Singapore in 2009 by
Institute of Southeast Asian Studies
30 Heng Mui Keng Terrace
Pasir Panjang
Singapore 119614

E-mail: publish@iseas.edu.sg
Website: <http://bookshop.iseas.edu.sg>

The responsibility for facts and opinions in this publication rests exclusively with the authors and their interpretations do not necessarily reflect the views or the policy of the publisher or its supporters.

ISEAS Library Cataloguing-in-Publication Data

Tawfik Ismail
    Malaysia's first year at the United Nations : as reflected in Dr Ismail's reports home to Tunku Abdul Rahman / compiled by Tawfik Ismail and Ooi Kee Beng.
    1. Ismail Dato Abdul Rahman, Tun, 1915–1973.
    2. United Nations.
    3. Malaysia—Foreign relations.
    I. Ooi Kee Beng, 1955–
    II. Title.
JZ4997.5 M3T23   2009

ISBN 978-981-230-902-0 (hard cover)
ISBN 978-981-230-903-7 (PDF)

Photo credit: Cover photo courtesy of The New Straits Times Press (Malaysia) Berhad.
Cover concept by Ooi Kee Beng
Typeset by Superskill Graphics Pte Ltd
Printed in Singapore by Utopia Press Pte Ltd

CONTENT

CHRONOLOGY OF TUN DR ISMAIL ALHAJ BIN DATUK ABDUL RAHMAN'S LIFE

1915 — Born 4 November in Johor Bahru to Abdul Rahman bin Yassin (1890–1970) and Zahara binte Abu Bakar (?–1936).

1922 — Starts his education at Sekolah Bukit Zaharah and later goes to English College, both in Johor Bahru.

1936–39 — Does medical studies at King Edward College of Medicine, Singapore.

1939–45 — Studies medicine at Queen's College, Melbourne University.

1945 — Becomes the first Malayan medical graduate from Melbourne University, and subsequently returns to Malaya in 1946. He joins the Medical Department in Johor, but leaves after a short stint.

1947–53 — Goes into private practice in Johor Bahru, and is moderately successful with a clinic called Tawakkal (Trust in God), named after his childhood home.

1948–54 — Nominated unofficial member of the Johor State Council, and then official member of the Johor Executive Council. He is elected into the Johor Bahru Town Council.

1950 — Marries Norashikin Seth (nickname Neno, born 17 January 1930 in Johor Bahru). The couple has six children, two girls and four boys (Mohd Tawfik Ismail, born 23 September 1951 in GH in JB; Zailah, born 2 May 1953 in GH in JB; Badariah, born 8 March 1957 in PJ; Mohamed Tarmizi, born 23 May

1960 in Bangsar KL; Zamakhshari, born 16 September 1964 at GH in KL, and Mohamed Ariff, born 25 October 1967 in KL).

1951 — Finally joins Umno after Onn Ja'afar resigned and Tunku Abdul Rahman had gained control of the party.

1953 — Appointed in September as unofficial member of the Federal Legislative Council under Sir Gerald Templer. He becomes Member of Lands, Mines and Communication upon Tunku Abdul Rahman's request. He moves with his family to Kuala Lumpur.

1954–55 — Becomes Member of Natural Resources.

1955 — Elected to the Federal Legislative Council for the Johore Timor constituency (to be re-elected in 1959, 1964 and 1969). Elected Minister for Natural Resources, and lays groundwork for Felda in May (see *The Star*, 26 March 2001).

1956 — Appointed Minister of Commerce and Industry by the new Chief Minister Tunku Abdul Rahman.

1957 (September) – 1959 (February) — Becomes Minister Plenipotentiary (without portfolio), and is sent as Malaya's first ambassador to Washington D.C., USA, and Malaya's first Permanent Head of Federation to the United Nations in New York.

1959 — Returns from Washington and continues to serve as Minister of Commerce and Industry.

1959 — Elected member for Johore Timor to the Dewan Ra'ayat and is appointed Minister of Foreign Affairs in August. He is Minister of Commerce and Trade from 20 September to 17 November.

1960 — Becomes Minister of Internal Security on 16 November, and also chairman of the Commission of the Enquiry into the Position of the Malayan Student Community in UK and the Republic of Ireland.

1961 — Given the additional post of Minister of Home Affairs on 22 February. Also appointed Federal Representative to the Internal Security Council in Singapore, until 16 September 1963.

1962 — Leads delegation to UN General Assembly 17th meeting.

1963 — Becomes chairman of Malaysian Security Board.

1964 — Re-elected member of Johore Timor Constituency in April. Appointed Minister of Home Affairs and Minister of Justice. In September, he leads a Malaysian delegation to the UN Security Council to debate Indonesian aggression.

1965 — Makes trip to United Nations Headquarters in New York with his wife Neno, together with Philip Kuok and wife, then travels to Madrid, London and Beirut, before returning home end of November. In September he is made in absentia Grand Officer of the National Order of Vietnam, by the South Vietnamese government through a visiting delegation.

1966 — He starts the year by visiting Manila to attend the presidential inauguration of Ferdinand Marcos. In April, he accepts an invitation from the South Korean Central Intelligence Service to visit Seoul for eight days, and is awarded the Order of Merit (First Class). He flies to London in May 1966 to attend the Conference of Law Ministers from the Commonwealth. He becomes chairman of Malayan Banking after its financial collapse and subsequent nationalization. He becomes the first to be conferred the Seri Setia Mahkota (Grand Commander), which carries the title "Tun".

1967 — In June, he resigns from the Cabinet — though not as MP — for health reasons, and returns to private medical practice. He joins the board of Malaysian Sugar Refineries, and Guthries.

1967 — Undergoes successful treatment at Royal Marsden Hospital in London for cancer of the naso-pharynx. Starts private practice in Kuala Lumpur with a group of doctors upon his return.

1969 — Asked to return to government by Tun Razak after 10 May elections. Becomes Deputy Director of Operations of the National Operations Council. On 12 June, he is appointed Minister of Home Affairs. In September, he makes a trip to Europe and the United Kingdom for medical treatment over three weeks. A medical check-up in 23–24 September gives him "a clean bill of health". His official golf handicap is certified by the Royal Selangor Golf Club, on 21 October, as 15.

1970 — Leaves for London on March 3 for heart consultation, and stays for nine weeks. In his absence, he is awarded the Republic of Indonesia Medal Second Class when President Suharto visited Kuala Lumpur. In September, the new premier Tun Abdul Razak bin Hussein appoints him deputy. He visits London between October 4 and 11 for a medical check-up on the way to New York for 25th anniversary celebrations of the United Nations.

1971 — Visits Dubrovnik, in September, he travels to Singapore to study Singapore's low-cost housing schemes. While visiting Sabah in May, he is awarded the Sri Panglima Darjah Kinabalu. He stays in London from 24 Oct–28 Nov for a medical check-up, returning to Malaysia *via* Paris, Belgrade and Cairo.

1972 — He receives the Honorary Fellowship Award from the Malaysian Institute of Management (MIM).

1973 — He takes on the portfolio of Minister of Trade and Industry on 3 January, and in March, visits Canberra, Sydney, Melbourne, Hobart and Armidale, with his wife and daughter Zailah, for talks regarding investments in Malaysia. He pays a visit to his alma mater, Queen's College, University of Melbourne, where he is conferred an honorary degree of doctor of laws. He also visits the University of New England in Armidale to see his son Tawfik Ismail. On 9 June, he is awarded a similar degree by Universiti Sains Malaysia. Malaysia's Academy of Medicine makes him Honorary Member. On Thursday 2 August, he passes away of a heart attack at his home on Maxwell Road (renamed Jalan Tun Dr Ismail in early 1974) in Kuala Lumpur. On Sunday 4 August, after the country's state funeral, he becomes the first to be buried at the State Mausoleum.

FOREWORD

I feel very honoured to be given the opportunity by the Institute of Southeast Asian Studies of Singapore to write a Foreword for its second publication on Tun Dr Ismail Abdul Rahman. I wish to congratulate the Institute for publishing this edition on the late Tun Dr Ismail, this time confined to his contributions to the evolution of the nation's foreign policy, based on his personal records, speeches, letters etc. The Institute, through its first publication — *The Reluctant Politician: Tun Dr Ismail and His Time* (2006) — has made all Malaysians aware of the role that Dr Ismail played in nation building. Now, with this volume — *Malaya's First Year at the United Nations, as Reflected in Dr Ismail's Reports Home to the Tunku* — the Institute gives the reader a complete profile of Dr Ismail as an astute diplomat and the formulator of foreign affairs who chartered the nation's course in international relations in the early years of its independence.

When I was appointed Foreign Minister in 1975 by Tun Razak, Malaysia's foreign policy continued to be built on the foundation and direction set by Dr Ismail. His writings and speeches, and his letters to the Tunku, covering a variety of foreign policy issues, are a valuable asset in understanding the unique role he played in the nation's history. He was without doubt the primary architect of Malayan (Malaysian) Foreign Policy.

As I read this manuscript, I am amazed by Dr Ismail's ability to transform himself very confidently into a successful diplomat at the United Nations when he was there as our first Permanent Representative. He was never trained as a diplomat. He was a politician and a medical doctor by training. He was also the Malayan diplomat to first address the United Nations when Malaya was admitted into the world body. During his tenure at the United Nations and as Ambassador to the United States, Dr Ismail succeeded in introducing the Federation of Malaya to the world in a dignified manner. The Tunku and his Cabinet colleagues were proud of his service to the nation.

His first speech to the United Nations is a testimony to his commitment to a multiracial Malaya, and it reveals the joy he felt over the fact that the nation had gained "the right and good fortune to live as a free, independent and united nation among the free nations of the world". His life-long service to the nation was recognized when he was later bestowed a "Tunship" by His Majesty, the Yang Di Pertuan Agong. The story of this illustrious son of Malaysia stands as a model for all Malaysians to emulate. As former Foreign Minister of Malaysia, I too am guided by his principles.

Tengku Tan Sri Dato' Seri Ahmad Rithauddeen
Former Foreign Minister of Malaysia
January 2008

PROLOGUE

Malaysia's first Permanent Head of Federation to the United Nations and first ambassador to the United States of America, Dr Ismail Abdul Rahman, kept relatively detailed notes about his experiences and thoughts during his 17 months in New York and Washington. This was done on his own initiative as he thought that it would provide Tunku Abdul Rahman Putra, Malaya's first Prime Minister and External Affairs Minister, with what could be useful information.

Just before Malaya gained independence from Great Britain on 31 August 1957, the Tunku had decided to send his faithful colleague Dr Ismail to the United States. He was convinced that the latter would provide the new state with competent representation at the world body, and in the most powerful nation in the world. Dr Ismail was excited by what he considered an honour, despite suspicions voiced by friends and relatives that he was being effectively "exiled" from the centre of Malayan politics. An understanding was apparently reached between Dr Ismail and the Tunku that the posting to the USA would be only for a year.

In July 1957, slightly over a month before Malaya's independence, he flew to the United States to secure three buildings for the embassy, and a lease for an office in New York. He returned in time for the celebration of independence, and left again on 5 September with his party which included Ismail Mohamed Ali — who was to be the economic minister at Malaya's Washington embassy — and "four women, nine children and thirty-one pieces of luggage". Three of these children — six-year-old son Tawfik Ismail, four-year-old daughter Zailah, and six-month-old daughter Badariah — belonged to the 42-year-old Dr Ismail and his 27-year-old wife, Norashikin (Neno) Seth.

Malaya became the 82nd member of the United Nations on 17 September 1957. The country's delegation was welcomed the following afternoon at the General Assembly's 678th meeting by the President of the 12th Session, Leslie Munro of New Zealand:

> It is very proper, on this happy occasion, that we should recall the record of the Federation of Malaya's uninterrupted progress towards independence, the great responsibility and statesmanship exercised by the Malayan leaders, and the harmony and co-operation existing between the Federation of Malaya and the United Kingdom, with whose guidance and help, the new State has taken its place in the community of nations.

John Selwyn Brooke Lloyd, the Secretary of State for Foreign and Commonwealth Affairs of the United Kingdom, Malaya's former colonial master, made the following point on that auspicious occasion:

> Some people have congratulated the Federation of Malaya on having won its fight for independence. Well, that fight was not against us, the British. We have, as a matter of deliberate policy, sought to guide the peoples of the British Empire to self-government and independence. We have not always agreed with them upon the timing or the precise methods, but it has been, and is, our declared and deliberate course of policy — a policy not forced upon us but voluntarily undertaken, and we are proud of it.

From what can be gathered from other sources, leading Malaya's delegation into the United Nations General Assembly Hall for the first time was one of Dr Ismail's proudest moments.

> Our admission to the United Nations was spectacular. We all dressed in the national costume — or at least those of us who had them. In addition, I had a kris tucked into my waist. This was the first time that a weapon of any kind had been brought into the General Assembly of the United Nations (Drifting c13).

His inaugural speech (Appendix 1) was relatively short. There were 40 foreign ministers present at that general debate, which, according to him, "certainly provided a wonderful opportunity for a foreign minister to gather facts with which to evolve a foreign policy for his Government". He later wrote in a letter to the Prime Minister's Office (PMO) that he thought it a pity that the Tunku was unable to be among them (Letter 18 December 1957).

Already the following week, more precisely on 24 and 25 September, Dr Ismail participated in the general debate during the General Assembly's 686th and 687th meeting (Appendix 2a and 2b). Busy as he was, he did not have cause or occasion to participate again until 26 September 1958 at the 761st meeting of the 13th Session (Appendix 4).

Dr Ismail thus "threw heart and soul" into his new job, but soon found out how much the double posting would demand of him and his young family. The lack of governmental preparation for the two missions, financially or otherwise, made things exceedingly stressful. He pointed out time and again to the Treasury that other newly independent countries were spending much more man-hours and money on their Washington and New York missions (Drifting c3).

About four months after arriving in the USA, Dr Ismail wrote to Oscar A. Spencer, economic adviser at the PMO, briefly informing him about working conditions at the embassy and of the mission in the first few months. He was also upset that the Treasury was giving him trouble over expenditure spent on setting up the two offices.

> My task is rendered the more difficult by the presence of, with the exception of Ismail [Ali], inexperienced, and in the case of our UN office in New York, mediocre staff. For the last three months my staff in Washington had to work in a building in which the work of renovating was going on at the same time, and I and my family had literally to camp with hired furniture in our Embassy, while waiting for it to be painted and furnished (Letters 18 December 1957).

His working day could last as long as 20 hours, and he had to commute between New York and Washington three to four times a week. Despite the workload, he conscientiously jotted down his experiences and thoughts whenever he could.

These "Notes by the Ambassador" starts from 30 December 1957 and ends on 21 August 1958. None exists from the first four months. This was probably due to the fact that Dr Ismail's party had difficulties settling in because of construction work at the residence. His "American diary" ends on 21 August 1958, and nothing seems to have been preserved beyond a few letters sent to the Tunku between then and 8 January 1959, when Dr Ismail's family sailed for home via Italy on the *Guilio Cesare*.

The accounts of his time in the USA were sent regularly "on a personal basis" to the Tunku. In a cover letter accompanying the first collection of remarks, dated 27 January 1958, Dr Ismail cautiously said that he would stop sending his "diary" if it did not prove useful to the prime minister. According to him, Ismail Ali was jotting down his own comments separately, and sending them to Ghazali Shafie, the permanent secretary at the External Affairs Ministry (Letters).

Ismail Ali was three years younger than Dr Ismail, and was known for his writing skills. Both were among the Malayan scholars cut off from all contact with Malaya during the Japanese occupation. Dr Ismail was doing his medical studies at Queen's College, Melbourne University, and did not return to Malaya until 26 July 1946. Ismail Ali studied economics at Cambridge on a Queen's Scholarship, and then went over to law studies, acted as firewatcher during German raids, worked for the British Broadcasting Corporation's Far Eastern Service, and finally taught the Malay language to military personnel at London University's School of Oriental and African Studies (SOAS). He returned to Malaya in late 1948 (Chung 2002).

The relationship between these two men — both highly exacting in their working style — was marked by mutual respect and mutual irritation (Interview, Lim Taik Choon, 13 May 2006). They both had a fondness for the fine arts and for literature, and it was Ismail Ali who pushed Dr Ismail to become a life-long member of the Book of the Month Club. During their stay in the USA, Ismail and his wife Neno paid frequent visits to art exhibitions, and their residence would acquire and display works by famous Malayan artists such as Yong Mun Seng and Arif. These remain among the more valuable items in the embassy's possession.

Dr Ismail's two missions worked with a twelve-hour time difference in relation to Kuala Lumpur, and he would send off coded and ciphered documents by 9pm so that the External Affairs Ministry would have them before 9am, Kuala Lumpur time. Replies from Kuala Lumpur were sent off before 5pm that same day, arriving at 5am, New York time (Interview, Zakaria Ali, 12 April 2006).

Dr Ismail demanded of his staff that the major American newspapers be made available to him every morning, and would hold night meetings with them at the end of long days at the office (Interview, Lim Taik Choon, 13 May 2006).

Malaya, which had agreed to attaining independence within the Commonwealth of Nations, joined the General Agreement on Tariffs and Trade (GATT) as its 37th member on 24 October 1957 (Sodhy 1991: 191). The bilateral Anglo-Malayan Defence Agreement (AMDA) was signed by the Tunku six weeks before independence to provide a security umbrella for the infant nation. However, he abstained from applying for membership for Malaya in the South-East Asia Treaty Organisation (SEATO), in what was perceived as a cautious tactical choice.

> The sense of security provided through the Anglo-Malayan Defence Agreement — with which Australia and New Zealand became associated — made it possible for independent Malaya to repudiate the idea of membership in SEATO, which might well have alienated a number of states in Asia with whom Malaya sought friendly relations, as well as suggesting to its sizeable Chinese community that the country was to become involved in an anti-Chinese combination (Leifer 1974: 47).

As some have pointed out, "since Malaya had unequivocally camped on one side of the East-West conflict, it also naturally behaved strategically as a minor "cold warrior" (Saravanamuttu 1983: 28).

The Tunku was suspicious of the Afro-Asian Non-Aligned Movement, although he did prioritise ties with Saudi Arabia and Egypt (Sheppard 1995: 116). Bilateral agreements between Britain, Malaya, Australia, New Zealand and Singapore led in 1971 to the formation of the Five Power Defence Arrangements (FPDA), which replaced the AMDA.

At the United Nations, Dr Ismail saw it as his job to take clear positions on international affairs in order that Malaya's standpoint could be made known. Where relations with the United States were concerned, he sought technological support and financial aid, and investments from what he termed America's "new capitalism" (in contradistinction to the "old capitalism" of Great Britain). He believed that this "new capitalism" would be less exploitative than had been the case with British investments.

After his return to Malaya in February 1959, Dr Ismail was made Malaya's alternate governor to the International Bank and Reconstruction and Development (IBRD) and the International Monetary Fund (IMF).

Following success at the General Elections in July 1959, he took over the position of External Affairs Minister from the Tunku. The basic policy Dr Ismail adopted on taking charge of Malaya's foreign relations was what he termed "an independent line, by which I mean that our stand on international problems should not be influenced by the policies of other countries, big or small" (Drifting). He spoke on 5 October 1959 at the United Nations General Assembly against China's occupation of Tibet, proclaiming that it showed "that colonialism is still rampant in our area in the world", and vehemently denying that the Malayan standpoint was dictated by the United States. A motion, known as the Irish-Malayan resolution, was tabled, but declaimed as one submitted by "lackeys" of the Americans and British (Jain 1984: 39–40).

He noted the following in his uncompleted autobiography "Drifting into Politics":

> I learned when I was in the United Nations — where in addition to being a member of the Commonwealth group we belonged also to the Afro-Asian group — that the surest way to get into trouble was not to have a definite policy of our own on foreign issues because then we would be at the mercy of others. Although our policy of moderation in the United Nations did not get the approval of many members of the Afro-Asian group, we were respected because our policy was definite, logical and consistent.

Besides giving intimate details about Dr Ismail and his thoughts from that period on nation-building and global politics, this volume makes use of the "Notes by the Ambassador" to elucidate the state of world politics in 1958, Malaya's first year on the world stage. Therewith are provided insights into the issues the new nation had to entertain when dealing with a world caught in post-colonial wars, and immersed in the proxy conflicts of the superpowers.

Dr Ismail would later profess that the experience he gained from his time at the UN served him well in September 1964 when he had to argue Malaysia's case against Indonesian aggression (see *Malaysia's Case in the United Nations Security Council* (MEA 1965). On that critical occasion, he dramatically brought captured weapons before the Security Council. These included a Danish-made Madsen mortar, a German-made automatic rifle, an equipment belt with a water bottle and medical packs with instructions for use in Indonesian, an Indonesian air force parachute with the smock and trousers marked with the place name "Bandung", a military helmet of a type not used by Commonwealth forces, and other minor items.

Although the Soviet Union stopped the resolution against Indonesia on that occasion, Dr Ismail's performance before the Security Council boosted Malaysia's stance, and won for the country the global attention and popular support that he had hoped for.

Keeping the background of his experiences at the UN in mind, and his distrust of communist regimes, scholars will find it easier to understand his famous flare-up at the Tunku in 1960 when the latter mentioned publicly, and without prior consultation with him, the External Affairs Minister, that Malaya had to recognize the People's Republic of China eventually. He almost resigned then from the government, and soon moved to become Minister for Internal Security, and then of Home Affairs.

His conviction that the neutralisation of Southeast Asia — to be guaranteed by Washington, Moscow and Beijing — was necessary for regional peace finally led to Malaysia's recognition of the People's Republic of China, and later formed the basis of what became known as The Razak Doctrine. He proposed his vision of a neutral Southeast Asia on 23 January 1968, when he was a parliamentary backbencher.

His notes, together with the many footnotes supplied, are meant to provide the reader with a quick introduction to the state of international affairs in 1958, and to some of the problems that Malaya's leaders wrestled with on the world stage in the first year of its life. It is hoped that scholars of international relations, political science, nation building, and the history of the United Nations, and of Malaysia, will find these to be informative and inspiring, and provide them with more understanding about later events.

A special word of thanks is owed to ISEAS Director K. Kesavapany for giving moral and financial support to this project; gratitude is also owed to ISEAS Library and its staff for providing access to important documents, and for competent and courteous help; and to Dr Johan Saravanamuttu for providing very useful advice along the way and for the access he provided to the UN speeches used herein.

Tawfik Ismail & Ooi Kee Beng

Plate 1 — Dr Ismail waves goodbye as he leaves Kuala Lumpur for the United States to make preparations for his term as Ambassador and United Nations representative, 15 July 1957 [*Courtesy of NSTP*].

Plate 2 — Dr Ismail, as Minister Plenipotentiary (without portfolio), takes leave of Tunku Abdul Rahman Putra to fly off to the United States to become Malaya's first Ambassador to Washington as well as Permanent Representative to the United Nations, 5 September 1957 [*Courtesy of NSTP*].

Plate 3 — Dr Ismail, Ismail Ali and Tunku Ja'afar listen to opening discussions at the United Nations 12th General Assembly, where the Federation of Malaya was admitted as the world body's 82nd member, 17 September 1957 [*Courtesy of NSTP*].

Plate 4 — Dr Ismail addresses the United Nations 12th General Assembly on Malaya's admission as the world body's 82nd member, 17 September 1957 [*Courtesy of NSTP*].

Plate 5 — Dr Ismail observes proceedings on his — and Malaya's — first day at the United Nations, 17 September 1957 [*Courtesy of NSTP*].

Plate 6 — Dr Ismail makes his first call on American Secretary of State John Foster Dulles, 21 September 1957 [*Courtesy of NSTP*].

Plate 7 — The flag of the Federation of Malaya (second from left) is raised for the first time outside the United Nations building in a simple ceremony. Dr Ismail is congratulated by the president of the 12th General Assembly, Sir Leslie Munro, Ambassador of New Zealand, 15 October 1957 [*Courtesy of NSTP*].

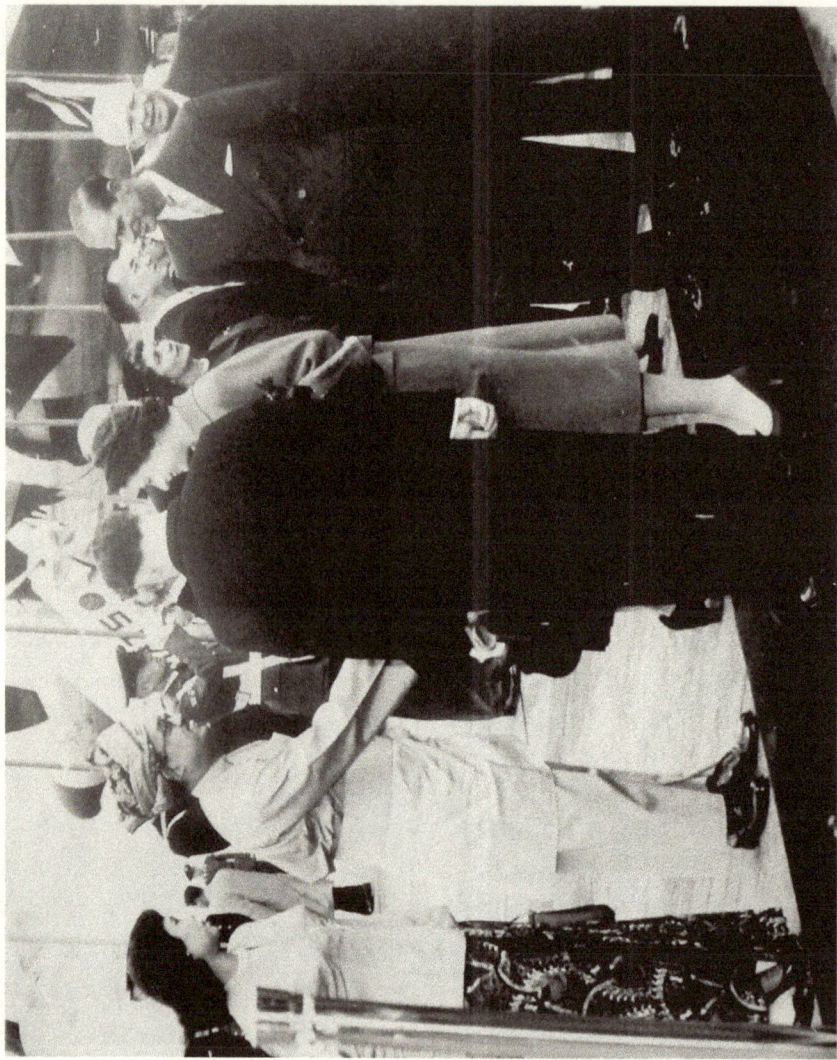

Plate 8 — Ismail and Neno greet Queen Elizabeth II (*centre*) on the English monarch's visit to the Washington, D.C. Her husband Prince Philip is behind her, and President Dwight Eisenhower is at far right. Strangely, Ismail did not mention this event in his regular reports to the Tunku, October 1957 [*Courtesy of NSTP*]

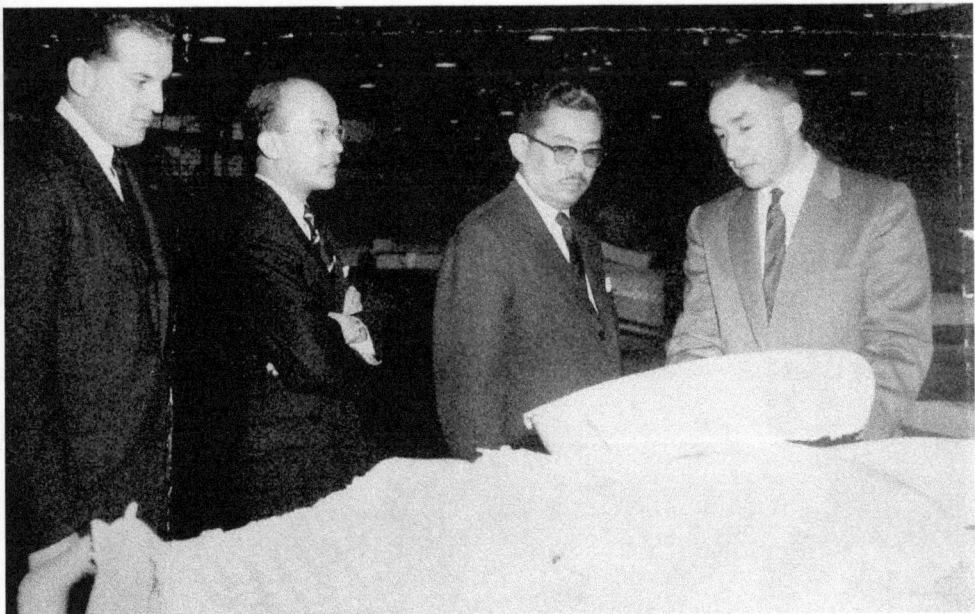

Plate 9 — Ismail and Ismail Ali (second from left) visit the Goodyear Tyre and Rubber Company at Akron, Ohio, March 1958 [*Courtesy of NSTP*].

Plate 10 — Dr You Chan Yang, Ambassador of South Korea, congratulates Dr Ismail on the occasion of Malaya's first anniversary. Norashikin and five-year-old Zailah look on, 31 August 1958 [*Courtesy of NSTP*].

Plate 11 — Norashikin bids farewell to Lady Munro, wife of the New Zealand
Ambassador, Sir Leslie Munro, who is nearing the end of his term in New York.
Dr Ismail arranged a party at the Malayan Embassy in their honour, 1 October 1958
[*Courtesy of NSTP*].

Plate 12 — Norashikin poses in the embassy garden in Washington, dressed in a kebaya of flowered Chinese silk in a rich shade of maroon, and a three-strand pearl necklace, 2 October 1958 [*Courtesy of NSTP*].

Plate 13 — A group picture taken on 10 January 1959 at the home of Eric Kocher (Director of the Office of Southeast Asian Affairs, US Department of State) and Mrs Kocher. Dr Ismail and Norashikin, and Mr Ourot R. Souvannavong (the Laotian Ambassador) and his wife, were the guests of honour. All four were leaving for their respective countries. Other guests at the informal dinner were Ambassador U Win of Burma, Ambassador Nong Kimny of Cambodia, Mr Robert Nathan, formerly a consultant to the Burmese government, and Mr William Sullivan, officer in charge of Burma Affairs, US Department of State, and their wives [*Courtesy of NSTP*].

Left to right, seated: Ambassador Nong Kimny, Dr Ismail, Ambassador U Win, Ambassador Ourot Souvannavong. Standing, left to right: Mrs U Win, Mr William Sullivan, Norashikin, Mrs Sullivan, Mrs Souvannavong, Mrs Kocher, Mrs Kimny, Mrs Robert Nathan and Mr Nathan, and Mr Eric Kocher.

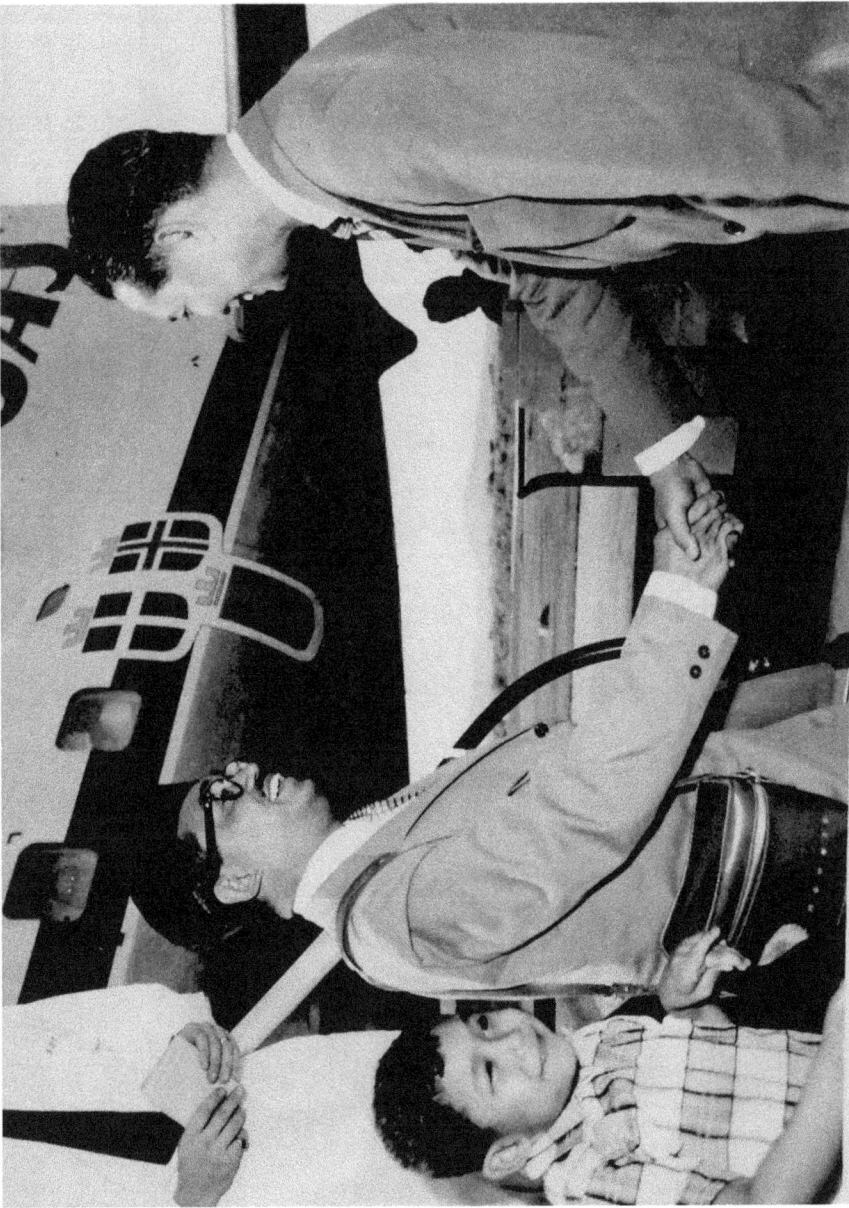

Plate 14 — Dr Ismail and his family returns to Kuala Lumpur and are greeted by his successor, Dato Nik Ahmed Kamil. Eight-year-old Tawfik Ismail is behind his father. Dr Ismail took over the position of External Affairs Minister on his return, 1 February 1959 [*Courtesy of NSTP*].

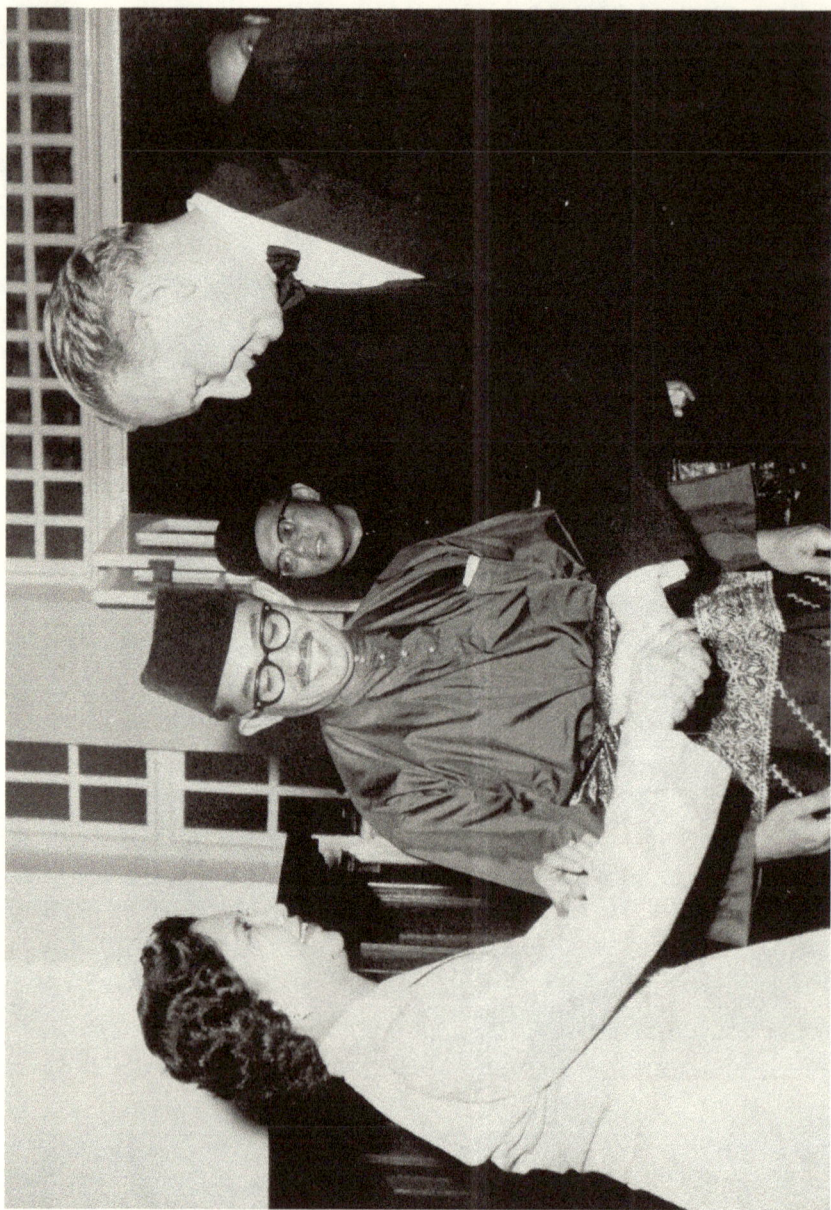

Plate 15 — Sweden's UN Secretary-General, Dag Hammarskjöld, arrives at a reception held in his honour by Dr Ismail and Neno at Istana Tetamu in Kuala Lumpur, soon after the couple had returned from New York, and Dr Ismail was made External Affairs Minister, 13 March 1959 [*Courtesy of NSTP*].

CONFIDENTIAL NOTES BY
THE AMBASSADOR

December 30 [1957] — Call on Ambassador Khoman of Thailand

Indonesia. Ambassador [Thanat] Khoman tried to persuade the Dutch to agree to talk with Indonesia, but the Dutch refused. When I told him that I was surprised at the pace with which the Indonesians had seized Dutch investments and that in doing so, had damaged the economy of Indonesia, Ambassador Khoman's opinion was that the Indonesians could not do otherwise. Indonesia has about 3,000 islands and if she wanted to do as she did, she must seize on the emotional issue generated by the West Irian question. She is further goaded by the Communists. He thought the U.S. and British Governments might help the Indonesians. I thought it unlikely because this will strain relationship with the Dutch and French. The U.S. would like to step in, but she is tied by NATO commitments.[1]

---

[1] When Indonesia won its independence in 1949, the Dutch government retained control over West Irian. Throughout the 1950s, Jakarta tried to regain the territory through the United Nations, and submitted the matter to the General Assembly in 1954. The Asia-Africa Conference passed a resolution in 1955 in support of Indonesia. The situation worsened to the extent that ties were severed between Indonesia and the Netherlands in 1961. The US did step in finally and sponsored talks in early 1962 between the Dutch and the Indonesians. These led to the New York Agreement that awarded control of West Irian to Indonesia which was in turn obligated to hold an election on self-determination in the territory no later than 1969.

Thanat Khoman became Thailand's deputy prime minister and foreign affairs minister later and was, in 1967, one of the five founding signatories of ASEAN. He was later awarded the highly respected title of "Tun" by the Malaysian government.

Afro-Asian Solidarity Conference. The Ambassador was afraid that a scheme might be hatched at this Conference, similar to that at the Calcutta Conference, with the purpose of advancing Communist aims in South-East Asia.[2]

Communist and Nationalist China. He thought that Malaya was wise not to recognise either of them. Cambodia, the Ambassador said, recognises both.[3]

Communism in Malaya. The Ambassador asked where the Communists in Malaya got their arms from. I said they were probably smuggled in. I further said that when Malaya was a dependency of the United Kingdom, which recognises Communist China, there was established the Bank of China which, no doubt, surreptitiously helps the Communist.[4]

---

[2] This took place in Cairo from 26 December 1957 to 1 January 1958. This Conference first met in April 1955 in Bandung, culminating as the first official summit of the Non-Aligned Movement in 1961, in Belgrade. The Calcutta Conference (also known as the Calcutta Youth Conference) refers to a meeting held in February 1948, during which directives were issued for Southeast Asian communists such as the Malayan Communist Party to take to armed struggle. This was organized by the newly formed Cominform (Communist Information Bureau, founded on 22 September 1947), whose worldview divided the world into two — an "imperialist camp" and an "anti-fascist camp".

[3] The refusal to recognize Beijing and Taiwan was purportedly to avoid complicating the domestic situation where the loyalty of many of Malaya's Chinese remained a politically sensitive issue. The communist regime in Beijing was recognized by Malaysia only on 21 May 1974, and as part of a larger policy initiated by Dr Ismail to achieve Southeast Asian neutralization.

[4] Dr Ismail would write to the Tunku on 10 September 1958 that "the Cabinet should make a decision to close the Bank of China immediately". He warned the Tunku that he had been receiving information that both in Indonesia and Burma, the bank had been financing political parties in past elections. The Tunku replied on 22 September to say that his civil servants, and in particular H.S. Lee, were advancing many reasons why the bank should not be closed down in Malaya. He would discuss the matter further with Dr Ismail once the latter was back home (Letters).

Following a series of events between China and Malaya throughout the second half of 1958 and early 1959, the Bank of China was asked to close operations by April 1, 1959. These events included a ban on the exhibition of Chinese goods at a Kuala Lumpur exhibition in July 1958, the imposition of special permits for the import of Chinese cotton piece-goods, and the prohibition on the import of four kinds of such products (Jain 1984: 35–37).

The Irish-Malayan UN resolution of October 1959 condemning the Chinese occupation of Tibet worsened relations between China and Malaya.

On Getting Together. The Ambassador expressed the wish that since Malaya and Thailand are such close neighbours, we should get together to discuss things which need not commit our Governments. I reciprocated his wish and said that this was also the fervent desire of our Prime Minister.[5]

January 6, 1958 — Call on the British Ambassador

Economics. We discussed the economic position of the USA and the Ambassador quoted a well-known economist (whose name was not mentioned) who said that although in the long run, for example, a period of 10 years, the USA economy may be balanced, in the intervening period it is subjected to fluctuations which have repercussions on world economy.

Politics — Disarmament. The Ambassador asked whether I read the U.K. Prime Minister's speech, to which I replied I had. His opinion was the same as that of his Prime Minister, i.e. that while the issues of deadlock between the Great Powers looked as insoluble as ever over the question of disarmament, there may arise some benefit from a meeting at the Foreign Ministers' level.

Communism. The Ambassador traced the history of Laos from the time of the Geneva Conference. It seems that since the leaders of Communists in Laos are related to those of the Government by blood, the present coalition may not suffer the fate of similar coalitions elsewhere. I said that Communists, if they are real Communists, place their loyalty to the Communist doctrine above everything else and, therefore, unless the Communists in Laos are false, the same fate will befall Laos as in other countries where such coalitions exist.

Call on the Afghanistan Ambassador

The Ambassador congratulated our Delegation to the last Session of the United Nations on its good work and, in doing so, he felt sure that he also expressed the sentiments of a number of other Delegations.

---

[5] Dr Ismail was later instrumental, as Home Affairs Minister, in establishing military cooperation with the Thai army in fighting communist guerillas along the Thai-Malaysian border.

The Indonesian Problem. The Ambassador was very sad at the turn of events in Indonesia. His Government had always supported Indonesia and would continue to do so, but he felt that the recent actions of Indonesia against the Dutch, which resulted in the violation of many international agreements between the two countries, have placed the Indonesians in an unfavourable light in the eyes of the world. The Ambassador, who was his country's first Ambassador to Indonesia, thought that much of the trouble which is now besetting that country is attributable to the fact that President Soekarno, whom he knew personally, had not taken an active part in the country's administration. In this respect the Ambassador compared the actions of Nehru with those of Soekarno and the relationship between India and Britain with that between Indonesia and the Dutch. Nehru, instead of becoming President, accepted the office of Prime Minister and thus is directly handling the administration. Because of his prestige, he was able to achieve moderation among the extremists. Soekarno did the opposite and as a result there was fighting and jealousy among the leaders as well as a rampant growth of corruption. India slowly liquidated British interests with no dislocation to her economy, whereas Indonesia by her action brought havoc to her own economy, albeit at the same time harming the Dutch.

Singapore. The Ambassador was interested to know the fate of Singapore. I told him the reasons why we could not take Singapore in.[6]

January 7, 1958 — Call on the Burmese Ambassador

Biography. The Ambassador was formerly the Minister-in-Charge of Planning in Burma and had served as his country's Ambassador to India in 1946. He good-naturedly recalled the days spent in India, when he was completely ignorant of Protocol and used to speak over the phone direct to Pandit Nehru, a custom no longer permitted in their present day Protocol-conscious India.

---

[6] These reasons were not recorded in writing, as far as can be ascertained.

Economics. I asked the Ambassador about the economic survey of his country. He said that under Point Four Programme, his country employed private firms of economic surveyors from America, of which one was named Nathan.[7] The surveys undertaken were of a similar nature to those carried out in Malaya by the World Mission. Apropos this subject of economic surveys, the Ambassador said that some firms have political affiliations. For example, Nathan is affiliated to the Democratic Party. As a result of this, Burma had some difficulties when it employed Nathan because at that time the Republicans had a big say in the financing of loan. He advised that if Malaya was interested in utilising American firms, she should either employ firms affiliated to the Party in power or firms run by men who once served in international agencies such as the World Bank, because such persons had developed business connections which are indispensable when the question of raising loans cropped up. The Ambassador discussed the difficulties of attracting private capital to Burma because of the socialistic policy of her Government. Even assurances that certain enterprises would never be nationalised were not enough. The Government is contemplating on the passing of legislation for the full expatriation of capital, tax holidays, etc., to provide further inducement to private enterprise. At present experts from America in the field of mining, commerce, etc., drawn from the State Department and Ministry of Commerce, are in Burma conducting surveys. In connection with American experts, the Ambassador remarked that they are "white elephants" because they are very expensive.

Political. We discussed the conditions in those countries which have gained their independence from the British and compared them with those who have achieved a similar status from other Colonial Powers and agreed that, although much could be said against the British type of colonialism, there was no denying the fact that Britain did more good to her colonies than

---

[7] The Point Four Programme is named after point four in President Harry Truman's inaugural speech made on 20 January 1949, which was purportedly an expansion of the Marshall Plan beyond Europe to cover the globe. It tied American foreign aid to the containment of global communism, and made governments — not social groups in developing countries — the recipients of such assistance.

other Colonial Powers.[8] In Burma at present there are not many political parties as in Indonesia. The present Government is run by the Anti-Fascist Peoples Liberation League Party and its members consist of socialists who have clearly listed which enterprises should be State-owned and which enterprises should be left for private entrepreneurs.

Communism. The Ambassador said Burma is well-nigh approaching the end of Communist insurgency. Last week about 200 Communists surrendered.

New Zealand

I lunched with the Ambassador of New Zealand, Mr. White, the Minister and Mr. Jeffrey of the New Zealand Embassy.

As the Ambassador was also the President of the United Nations General Assembly at the 12th Session, the conversation naturally opened on whether there would be a Special Session of the Assembly.[9] The Ambassador thought that there would probably be a request in this direction and, if supported by a large majority, the Assembly would be called into Session. He asked how many among the Afro-Asian countries would vote for it. I said that Malaya, Laos, Cambodia, Thailand, the Philippines, Pakistan and probably Ceylon would vote against. The Ambassador was also interested in the future of Brunei, Sarawak and North Borneo. I said that in the long run there was bound to be a confederation of independent States which were under British colonialism and that if such a confederation materialised, then probably the problems of Singapore would be solved; Mr. White was further interested in knowing how we would proceed with the publicity of Malaya in the USA. New Zealand, in spite of the efforts made by its Embassy, is not getting very much publicity. I informed him that we were in no hurry to publicise our country and that in some respects we were in a more fortunate position than New Zealand. For example, the communist terrorism in Malaya had aroused

---

[8] Burma, unlike most other former British colonies, did not join the Commonwealth when it gained independence on 4 January 1948.
[9] Besides being ambassador to the USA, Leslie Munro was also New Zealand's permanent representative to the UN.

interest in America about Malaya and had resulted in publicity without our own effort.

Thai Embassy — Cocktail Reception (to bid farewell to Mr. Young of the State Department)

Mr. Whittington of the State Department informed me that the American Ambassador in Kuala Lumpur was discussing the question of a loan for development purposes with the Alliance Government.

Call on the Ambassador of France

Disarmament. France is interested in having a meeting of diplomats of the Soviet bloc and the Western Powers to discover whether there are grounds on which a meeting of Foreign Ministers of these two blocs could usefully take place. He believed that a strong West would succeed in influencing the Soviet attitude.

January 9, 1958 — Call on the Libyan Ambassador

There is not much to be recorded except that the Ambassador traced the history of his country which was very interesting.

Attended Congress to listen to the President's Speech

Judging by the applause which greeted his speech, evidently the President still enjoys the confidence and love of the Congress.[10] In contrast to our own Legislative Council, Members of Congress are not afraid to show their emotions. The President appeared to be in good health at the beginning of his speech, but his voice became hoarse towards the end which I thought could not wholly be explained by the length of his speech which lasted $3/4^{th}$ of an hour.

---

[10] This was President Dwight D. Eisenhower, who had been re-elected and was just about to begin his second term.

January 10, 1958 — Call on the Ambassador of Sweden

The Ambassador was late for the appointment and was profusely apologetic. There was more warmth in his manner and speech than the other Western Ambassadors on whom I made my official call. Sweden, said the Ambassador, was highly industrialised and, in answer to my question regarding his country's attitude towards the Free Trade Area, he informed me that Sweden always followed Great Britain with whom she had important trade relations.

Return Call by the Ambassador of Saudi Arabia

The Ambassador made a call with his wife at our Embassy. He was deeply interested in our Kelantan silver in which we served the cakes and coffee. He had returned from a holiday in Florida and said that the place was full of Jews. He asked whether there were many of them in Malaya and I replied that there was only a handful.

January 11, 1958

Arrived in New York at 11.45 a.m. and was met by Tunku Ja'afar [first secretary at Malaya's UN mission]. Went to our Mission where I saw Lim Teow Chong and Zain. Tunku Ja'afar revived the subject of a five-day week for our office on the ground that such work as attending official functions, which our officers in America had to do and which officers in Malaya did not undertake, should be counted as part of office work.

In the evening, I and my wife attended a reception and dinner given by the American Nobel Anniversary Association. Among the distinguished guests were Mr. Lester Pearson, Lord Boyd Orr, Pearl Buck, Sir Leslie Munro and Szent-Georgi.[11] Mr. Lester Pearson made a stimulating address, but

---

[11] Pearson became Canadian Prime Minister in 1963 and was recipient of the Nobel Peace Prize in 1957 for his mediating role for the UN, over the Suez Canal Crisis. This crisis came about when Egypt nationalized the canal on 26 July 1956 and was attacked by Britain, France and Israel a few months later. The Scottish Lord Orr was given the Peace Prize in 1949 for his work on human and animal nutrition. American Pearl S. Buck won the Literature Prize in 1938. The Hungarian, Albert Szent-Györgyi, who later became a Swedish citizen, received the Nobel Prize in Physiology or Medicine in 1937 for his discovery of, and work on, vitamin C. New Zealander Leslie Munro was president of the 12th UN General Assembly (1957–58).

offered nothing new to what had already been said by the leaders of both the Western and Soviet blocs, except to say that the question of good faith, in his view, would be revealed when the talks began. Lord Boyd Orr was the next speaker who stirred the interest of those present. On disarmament, among other propositions which had been aired by many other men beside himself, he said that Poland's proposal for a neutral zone in Europe where no nuclear bombs should either be stored or manufactured was originally made by Sir Anthony Eden.[12] On China, he stated that once she became industrialised and started manufacturing her own atomic bombs, she would not be subservient to any country.

The other speakers said nothing that was not common knowledge.

January 13, 1958

Delivered a lecture on Malaya to the Pan-Pacific Women's Association at the Woodrow Wilson Foundation, East 65 St., Park and Madison Avenue, which was followed by a one reel film show on Merdeka. At question time, among other questions, firstly information was sought on what percentage of the Chinese resident in Malaya before Merdeka became automatically citizens of independent Malaya and secondly the reasons for the exclusion of Singapore from the Federation.[13]

---

[12] Robert Anthony Eden was British Prime Minister from 1955 to 1957, and is mainly remembered for his role in the Suez Canal Crisis. American opposition to the invasion led to a retreat by the invaders. The outcome of the crisis is often used to mark the end of British global power, the way the defeat at Dien Bien Phu signaled the end of French colonialism.

[13] These figures were probably not available to Ismail at that time. An indirect indication of the volume of Malayan Chinese who became citizens after 1959 is seen in the fact that they made up only 11.2% of the total electorate in 1955, but by 1959, they comprised 35.6% of the voters (Andaya & Andaya 1982: 268).

With the fall of British Malaya to the Japanese in 1942, the Straits Settlements disappeared and the polity was not revived when the British returned in 1945. Instead, the Malayan Union was formed that included all parts of the peninsula except Singapore, which was retained as a crown colony. This separation continued under the Federation of Malaya agreement made between Malay leaders and the British in 1948. Malaya and Singapore remained separate beyond Malaya's independence in 1957 and Singapore's gaining of self-government in 1959. Only on 16 September 1963 did they come together along with Sabah and Sarawak to form Malaysia. Singapore remained in the federation for only two years, and left to become an independent state on 9 August 1965.

January 14, 1958

In the morning went to the Meta T.V. Studio to participate in a show on Malaya for the benefit of school children. I was asked questions on the Emergency in Malaya and on our problems of development.[14]

I had lunch with Warren Lockwood, who had recently paid a visit to Malaya. Mr. Lockwood said that he had general discussions with the Prime Minister and discussions in detail with the Minister for Commerce & Industry, to whom he had made definite proposals, and who promised to go into the matter with me. Lockwood showed me a letter from Loch of the Ministry of Commerce & Industry to the effect that as the Minister would be away in Geneva and as he had to discuss the matter with his other colleagues, it would be some time before Lockwood could get an answer. Mr Lockwood was anxious to know something soon. I told him that I had not heard from the Minister for Commerce & Industry on the proposals he had advanced, but if he would let me have a copy I would study the matter with our Minister in Washington and try to get a definite reply from the Minister for Commerce & Industry. Lockwood said that his idea was to attract private capital from such well-known industrial firms as Ford, Rockefeller and steel manufacturers to be invested in Malaya. He is competent to do this because of his connections. He casually mentioned that he was going to have breakfast with Mr. Conlon, whom I saw in Washington. According to Mr. Conlon, Lockwood is associated with a firm doing publicity work. Evidently his firm is reputable.

January 16, 1958

Made calls on the Ambassadors of Denmark, the Netherlands and Switzerland.

The Ambassador of Netherlands asked questions on the Emergency in Malaya along what [are] now "customary" lines to which I gave "stock" replies. He knows Indonesia very well, having taken part in the negotiations which finally led to the transfer of sovereignty. He also knows Dr. Ali Sastromidjojo closely and is emphatic that Dr. Ali is not a Communist but

---

[14] The Emergency was declared by the British on 18 June 1948, and was immediately followed by increased violence perpetuated by members of the Malayan Communist Party. It officially ended in July 1960.

an embittered man because his belief in working with the Indonesian Communists, whom he considered to be different from other Communists just because they are Indonesians, has landed him in trouble both with the USA and the Communists. In the USA he is branded as a Communist or at the very least a pro-Communist. In Indonesia, his association with the Communists has brought him under their control — the reverse of what he expected. The Ambassador has a very high regard for Hatta who, he regretted, has not the same popular appeal as Soekarno. He said that his relationship with the Indonesian Ambassador has always been friendly since each of them asks a third person to say any unpleasant things which had to be said.[15]

January 17, 1958

The Ambassador of Thailand returned my call. He enquired whether there would be a fresh talk on the Communist trouble on the Malayan-Thailand border. I said that all I knew was that, from the statements of our Prime Minister which appeared in the Malayan newspapers, the Prime Minister considered it an insult to Thailand to offer rewards to Thai subjects for the capture of Communist-terrorists on the Thailand side of the border and that he expected to have talks with Thailand on co-operation at the border. Thailand agreed with the views of the Prime Minister on the offer of rewards since the Emergency is a Malayan problem.

I paid a visit to the Ambassador of Morocco, who is a skin specialist. He represented his country at UN from the time of her admission until last year. Because of his strong advocacy of anti-colonialism at the UN he was labelled as an extremist. His opinion of the Afro-Asian Solidarity meeting at Cairo is that it is an endeavour to achieve those objectives which could not be fulfilled at the Bandung Conference. At the Bandung Conference, the representatives spoke for their respective Governments and as a result India,

---

[15] Sastroamidjojo was twice premier of Indonesia (1953–55; 1956–57), and is often credited as a major proponent of the Conference of Asian and African states, which led to the Bandung Conference of 1955. He was also his country's permanent representative at the UN. When the Federation of Malaysia was being formed in the 1960s, he was one of the major figures supporting Soekarno's policy of confrontation against it.

Mohamed Hatta was Indonesian vice president in 1945–56 under President Soekarno. After resigning, he quickly became a major critic of the president.

Ceylon and Burma differed in their views from those of the other countries. In Cairo the representatives would be representing the people. I cannot but gain the impression that the Arab-bloc was dissatisfied with the "lukewarm" treatment which the Arab problems were receiving from the Afro-Asian bloc.

The Ambassador assumed that the Federation [of Malaya] would support the Arab countries in the Afro-Asian group and in her dealings with international affairs.

The Ambassador of Ghana paid a courtesy call. Evidently, his Embassy is labouring under the same difficulties as ours — having to read of events occurring in Ghana in the USA newspapers in the absence of direct information from his Government and having to camp in his Embassy while waiting for it to be furnished as well as to be staffed adequately — although in contrast to ours his Embassy already has an Information Officer.[16] He has written to his Prime Minister of his embarrassment and to his Information Department to send daily cablegrams of happenings in Ghana.

In the evening I gave a dinner to some of the Asian Ambassadors. After the dinner, Eric Kocher mentioned to me about a US$20 million loan asked for by [Commerce and Industry Minister] Tan Siew Sin, the negotiation on which is fairly advanced, and of a US$60 million loan sought by [Deputy Prime Minister and Defence Minister] Razak for Kampong Development in a cablegram sent by the American Ambassador to the State Department.[17]

January 20, 1958

Called on the Ambassadors of Korea, Ceylon and Japan.

The Ambassador of Korea

He is a Doctor of Medicine by profession and has had an extensive practice in Honolulu, where, according to him, he "even attended to Movie stars",

---

[16] The Malayan Embassy at 2401 Massachusetts Avenue, Washington D.C., underwent renovations in the first months of Ismail's stay. His family developed skin diseases during that trying period.
[17] Kocher was the director of Southeast Asian Affairs in the American State Department, to whom all requests for American aid from Southeast Asian governments would be made. He was also the US Consul-General to Kuala Lumpur in 1953–55.

before he was called upon by President Syngman Rhee, who was his former teacher and has been his close friend ever since, to be his country's ambassador to the USA.[18]

He says he is reputed as being outspoken against the USA, but actually he is a great friend of the USA, and he considers it a privilege for good friends to be outspoken. He wanted to buy the present Malayan Embassy, but his country could not afford it.[19]

The Ambassador of Ceylon

The Ambassador saw me accompanied by his Counsellor, which is very unusual in courtesy calls. However, to be fair, he prefaced the meeting by saying that since he knows me so well, the formalities of a courtesy call could be dispensed with and that he would take the opportunity to discuss matters.

He complimented me on the performance of our UN Delegation and said that his opinion was shared by other delegations, with whom he had talked. He seemed very interested in Dato' [E.E.C.] Thuraisingham and thought the Federation could very well make use of his services. I said that since he belonged to a rival political party and held a very important position in that party which was opposed to the Alliance, it was very difficult, much as we would have liked it, to give him an important position in the present Government set-up. He suggested making him an Ambassador.[20]

---

[18] The South Korean Ambassador was Dr You Chan Yang. Syngman Rhee was South Korea's first president, and held the office from 1948 to 1960. He resigned in 1960 in the face of the student-led April 19 Movement, and was whisked away from a lynch mob into exile in Hawaii.

[19] This last remark would have pleased Ismail, who had been having some trouble getting his purchase of embassy buildings approved by the Malayan Cabinet.

[20] E.E.C. Thuraisingham was a prominent Malayan lawyer and was Member for Education in the Federal Executive Council in the early 1950s. He was the first leader of the Ceylon Federation of Malaya and was made senator in 1957. He was a close friend of Onn Ja'afar, the founder of the United Malays National Organisation (UMNO) who resigned from the party in 1951 after its members refused to open it to non-Malay membership. Tunku Abdul Rahman took over the presidency with the support of Ismail and his brother Suleiman, among others. Onn went on to form the multi-racial Independence of Malaya Party (IMP), and later the Malay-based Parti Negara.

The Ambassador of Japan

The Ambassador recollected having met me in Tokyo in 1955 at the ECAFE meeting.[21] He had served in London but this was his first assignment to America. He was keen to know whether it was possible to increase Malayan trade with Japan and whether his country could be given the most favoured nation treatment. I told him that the Ministry of Commerce & Industry was looking into the question of trade agreements between Malaya and other countries.

January 21, 1958

Called on the Ambassador of Tunisia, who is also his country's representative to the United Nations. His Chancery is in a hotel called Hotel Roosevelt, but his country has purchased an Embassy for him. He talked English haltingly, having learnt it only during the last four months. His French, of course, is excellent. He said that newly independent countries must look more towards one another than to the "old" countries. Since he is one of the chief spokesmen at the UN General Assembly on the question of Algiers, I asked him whether this matter could not be solved on the pattern of the Commonwealth of Nations. He said that, in fact, his President is going to put forward this proposal on condition that the French accept the chief attributes of the Commonwealth, that is [that] the power to opt out of the Commonwealth must be vested in each member independently.[22]

In the evening, I and my wife attended a "good-bye" function held by the Ambassador of Australia and Lady Spender at the Australian Embassy. There was a very large attendance and the common topic was how sad everyone was at the departure of the Spenders — a tribute to the popularity of the couple.

---

[21] ECAFE stands for the United Nations' Economic Commission for Asia and the Far East. This regional arm of the world body was founded in 1947, and has been known since 1974 as the Economic and Social Commission for Asia and the Pacific (UNESCAP or ESCAP).

[22] The so-called Battle of Algiers started in September 1956, leading to a brutal war between French forces and the Algerian National Liberation Front (FLN). A general strike was called in 1957 to coincide with the UN debate on the issue.

In the middle of the function, my wife fainted and was unconscious for half an hour. She was attended to by Dr. and Dr. Lattimer, who were guests at the function. Poor woman! She has had a busy day today, having to receive and make calls on three Ambassador's wives with shopping for the Embassy thrown in between. It seems that if my wife has to do onerous official duties as an Ambassador's wife, then she should be entitled too to enjoy the pleasant duties of an Ambassador such as accompanying him on official tours. In fact this is what I intend to do, unless I receive instructions to the contrary.

January 24, 1958

The Ambassador of France made a return call on me. The conversation turned on the subject of economics. In reply to a question from me, the Ambassador said that the loan sought by his Government was for an entirely different purpose from that for which the Indian Government needed it. The French loan was to restore confidence in the Franc, whereas the Indian one was for "recurrent" expenditure. The Ambassador was optimistic that the slackness in the American economy would be set right towards the second half of this year.

In the evening, I and my wife attended the celebration of Independence Day by Libya. I got into a very interesting conversation with the Ambassador of Cambodia, and Mr. Nugroho of the Indonesian Embassy. The former was greatly impressed with the film on Merdeka celebrations, which I showed after a dinner at our Embassy which he attended. He was especially impressed by the scene which depicted the departure of the High Commissioner at Kuala Lumpur airport. This scene, according to the Ambassador, displayed the spirit of goodwill which existed between Great Britain and Malaya on the attainment of independence compared to the French and the Dutch. He considered the British a great people who knew when to give in gracefully and thereby to cement new ties. Mr. Nugroho said that when he was in England, he was struck by the sportive spirit of the English school-children who were taught to accept defeat gracefully. He said that in India and Pakistan he still saw pictures of the Queen and other members of the British Royalty hanging on the walls of homes, a thing which the Indonesians could never do with the pictures of the Dutch Royal family. According to him, this reflected the spirit which existed between Britain as a colonial power and her colonies on attaining independence. Had the Dutch in 1945, or even in 1950, displayed the spirit which Great Britain did on the independence of India, Pakistan and Malaya, the relationship between Indonesia and Holland would have been the same as that which now existed between Great Britain and her former colonies. According to him, Great Britain is a big nation, whereas Holland is like a small shopkeeper who kept on counting his pennies for ever.

January 26, 1958

I missed sending the Australian Ambassador and Lady Spender off by the afternoon Congressional train. This was rather unfortunate. My watch, which is self-winding, was losing half an hour and I, therefore, arrived at the Station ten minutes too late instead of a quarter of an hour earlier than the departure time of the train. The chauffeur had arrived at the Embassy at 2 o'clock and since he had the time-table of my activities with him, he could have reminded me. Alas, although he is a good chauffeur, he is deficient in grey matter and can only do what he is told. His basic salary is the equivalent of $800 Malayan!

January 27, 1958

Called on the German Ambassador.[23] He has been in the United States for six years and is leaving to take up a new appointment as an executive in the European Council formed as a result of the birth of a Common Customs Union between the six nations. The Ambassador is very enthusiastic about his new assignment. He looked upon the Council of Europe as a big step forward in abolishing jealousy and suspicion between France and Germany. He was equally vehement in denouncing Russia on her domination over East Germany. According to him, only a handful of German Communists are working with the Russians. When I told him that we are recruiting German

---

[23] Heinz (Heinrich) Ludwig Hermann Krekeler.

engineers, he said that he was pleased but that, in the long run, we must train our own people; otherwise independence would be incomplete.

January 28, 1958

Called on Mr. Robertson, Assistant Secretary of State (Far Eastern Affairs). A record of this interview has been transmitted to Dato' Razak under top secret cover.

January 29, 1958

Called on the Ambassadors of Argentina, Nicaragua and Bolivia. The Ambassador of Nicaragua is the Dean of the Diplomatic Corps.[24]

The Ambassador of Bolivia, who is serving his second term of office in America, was very interested in the International Tin Agreement and in the trade in Zinc and Lead. When I told him that part of the difficulties facing the Tin industry was the unloading of Russian Tin on the market, he wanted to know whether the State Department in Washington was aware of it. He told me that he had been, and would keep on, telling the State Department the virtue of extending help to countries suffering from economic distress in the "cold war" at the right time. According to him, the Communist tactic is just to cripple the economy of a country and then to offer economic aid.[25] It would then be almost impossible for such a country to refuse the aid. It was, therefore, far better for the USA to offer her economic aid before a country's economy was crippled. The Ambassador said that Bolivia used to occupy the second place among the tin producing countries; her production then was 40,000 tons a year. Now she is placed third after Malaya and Indonesia, her production being only 24,000 tons.

---

[24] This title is reserved for the longest-serving among ambassadors to a given country, in this case the USA.

[25] Interestingly, Ismail seemed to agree strongly with this line of thought (see Appendix 3). When he became Home Affairs Minister in 1961, his expressed strategy for fighting communist subversion was two-sided: prevention of subversion and economic development to minimize support for the communists. He was often worried that if the military battle against subversion went so far that economic development was hampered, the communists would benefit.

I had lunch with Colonel Goodfellows. He was head of the O.S.S. in the Army, which is a Department of Intelligence.[26] He belongs to a class of military personnel who, on retirement from active service, set themselves up as businessmen. They are engaged either by Governments or business firms to do specific jobs. For example, a Swiss firm bought an oil concession in Egypt from an American firm who, because of competing claims between its interest in Egypt and Saudi Arabia, decided not to work the former much to the consternation of the Egyptian Government. The Swiss firm, having no experience in drilling, engaged Colonel Goodfellows, who employed a firm experienced in oil drilling, working under his supervision.

According to Colonel Goodfellows, the results of oil-drilling in this part of Egypt, on the Sinai Peninsula to be exact, are beyond expectation. They have discovered a large oil bearing area which would surpass the areas in Saudi Arabia. If this is true, then Egypt's economic plight would be partly relieved, and it also accounts partly for Israel's invasion of the Sinai Peninsula and Britain's attack of Egypt on the Suez question.

In answer to Colonel Goodfellows' queries, I briefed him on the industrial potential of Malaya and on the Alliance policy of attracting foreign capital.

In the afternoon, I talked to Mr. Laidlaw, a representative of the "Straits Times" in Washington, over the telephone. He said that from January to October of last year, the Russians unloaded on the market 6,400 tons of tin and from October to January the total amount was over 12,000 tons. The tin is mined in the Caucasus and rural region of Russia and some of it came from China. The quality is inferior to Malayan tin. It is marketed in Denmark and distributed to such countries as Germany, Holland and the U.K., among others. The motive is not clear. It may be that Russia needs foreign exchange. On the other hand, she may want to depress the price of tin, thus aggravating the situation caused by a recession in trade in America as well as by the consumers' "Wait and see" policy in the hope that prices will go down still further.

[26] The Office of Strategic Services was the precursor of the Central Intelligence Agency of the USA, founded in June 1942 to supply the American Chiefs of Staff with strategic information about the Axis powers, and was disbanded on 20 September 1945.

January 30, 1958

I attended a meeting of Heads of Missions to the United Nations at the office of the Permanent Mission of the U.K. to U.N.

On disarmament, the Head of the U.K. Mission, Sir Pierson Dixon, said that the view of the U.K. Government was that it would be a mistake to have a meeting of the Disarmament Commission before a definite agenda was fixed. The Acting Head of the Pakistan Mission said that his information was that the Russians were veering to the view that if a summit meeting was held, they would be prepared for a compromise on substance. The conclusion of the meeting was that there should be no meeting of the UN on disarmament in the immediate future.

The second subject discussed was the Afro-Asian Solidarity Conference. The Head of the U.K. delegation frankly said that the view of London was that the Conference was Communist inspired. It was different from the Bandung Conference, in that at the Bandung Conference the Government of a country was represented while at Cairo it was the "people's representatives". Some of them, as in the case of Cyprus and Iraq, were persons who did not even reside in the countries they represented. The Indian representatives said too much must not be made of this Conference and that in India the reception accorded to it by the Government and newspapers was cool.

The final subject discussed was the composition of the General Committee and Committee Chairmanships. It was generally agreed that the growing custom of canvassing for candidacy for these posts one year, or in some cases two years, ahead of time was to be deplored. New Zealand brought up the matter of her intention to submit her candidacy to ECOSOC and hoped that she would receive the support of the Commonwealth countries.[27]

January 31, 1958

I went to have lunch with Mr. Bugbee, President of the Natural Rubber Bureau, and Mr. Ormsby, President of the Rubber Traders Association, at the Union League Club. The object of the luncheon was to make arrangements

---

[27] ECOSOC = United Nations Economic and Social Council.

for my visit to the rubber manufacturing factories at Akron. It was agreed that the visit should take place either in the week following the 10th of March or that after the 17th of March.

The subject of natural and synthetic rubber was discussed. Mr. Ormsby said that the impression that synthetic rubber manufacturers were purposively keeping the price of synthetic rubber low, in order to depress the price of natural rubber, was wrong. What actually happened, according to him, was that synthetic rubber was sold on the same principles as the natural product, i.e. the price does not fluctuate according to the supply and demand, but depends on the cost of production. He said that if the cost of production of natural rubber could be lowered, natural rubber would sell more than the synthetic in the future, particularly since the cost of labour is rising in America.

Bugbee was at great pains to impress on me and later Tunku Ja'afar that it would be a mistake for Malaya to agree to a rubber restriction scheme for two reasons. Firstly, because of her replanting programme, Malaya would be an efficient producer and any restriction would defeat the object she was aiming at. Secondly, any restriction would be retaliated by a greater production of synthetic rubber.

In the evening, I attended the Roosevelt Day Dinner with my wife, and among the principal speakers was Mr. Adlai Stevenson.[28] Mr. Adlai Stevenson is a beautiful speaker and the main theme of his speech was that America must not only depend on armed peace, but she must also take the initiative in the economic field to match or even surpass the Soviet achievement.

As the guests of Mrs. Roosevelt, among whom I and my wife were fortunate enough to be included, were seated in alphabetical order, I was lucky to sit on her left.

February 1, 1958

Spent the morning working in the office, as I had done in between engagements since my arrival in New York on 29th January.

---

[28] Stevenson was the presidential candidate for the Democratic Party in 1952 and 1956, both times losing to Dwight Eisenhower. He became Ambassador to the UN in 1961–65.

The office is working more smoothly since my last visit. Everyone is doing his allotted task. The staff petitioned that the office hours were longer, compared to those of other Missions. I asked Tunku Ja'afar to investigate into the matter. Tunku Ja'afar complained of lack of officers to help him. Although I agreed that his complaint was justified, I thought he himself could put in more work if he were prepared to carry some of his work home.

February 2, 1958

I decided to remain in New York rather than go back to Washington, because it was less costly and less tiring.

February 3, 1958

I gave a lunch to the Secretary-General of the United Nations and five of his colleagues, who were going to Kuala Lumpur for the ECAFE Conference at the Brussell Restaurant and the total of the bill was US$125.[29]

The conversation was general. The Secretary-General thought that the Arab Union may take the form of the Malayan Federation.[30]

February 4, 1958

Paid a return call to the Ambassador of Ghana, Mr. Daniel A. Chapman. Reminded the Ambassador of the dinner to be given by the Dean of the Diplomatic Corps on 18th February, which he evidently had forgotten, and he was very thankful for the reminder. The Ambassador deplored the current tendency in his country for politicians going at each other's throat in the

---

[29] Dag Hjalmar Agne Carl Hammarskjöld of Sweden was UN Secretary-General in 1953–61. He died in an air crash which led to endless speculation that his demise was the result of a conspiracy. At the time of his death, he had already been chosen to receive the Nobel Peace Prize for 1961. It was uniquely awarded to him posthumously.

[30] The Arab Union referred to here was most probably the United Arab Republic (UAR) formed between Egypt and Syria on 1 February 1958, with Gamel Abdel Nasser of Egypt as president. It collapsed in 1961.

fight for power. He had been Secretary to the Cabinet and remembered the days when there were only two parties — the Gold Coast Nationalists and the British Colonial Power. Creech-Jones, who was at that time the Secretary of State for Colonies, said that there would be no independence for the Gold Coast unless there were opposition parties. To meet this condition, opposition parties were artificially created. Now they have come to stay and have become a real nuisance.

Made a call on the Ambassador of Colombia, who had presented his credentials five days earlier than I did.

My wife developed a sore throat with high temperature. In spite of this, she accompanied me to a reception to celebrate the tenth anniversary of Ceylon's Independence because she had previously, on another occasion, cancelled a luncheon appointment with the Ambassador and his wife at the last moment due to illness. After the reception, we went to a dinner at the Indonesian Embassy in honour of the newly appointed American Ambassador to Indonesia, Mr. Howard Jones, and Mrs. Jones.

February 5, 1958

Received a return call from the Ambassador of Iraq, Mr. Shabandar, at the Chancery. The Ambassador said that two things could be interpreted from the events now involving Egypt and Syria. It might be a genuine get-together, which would be good for Arab unity. However, by by-passing Jordan and Lebanon, this assumption could not be true. It might be Communist inspired, in which case it would be very bad indeed. The Ambassador thought that the events must be weighed solemnly. If it is a move between Egypt and Syria prior to attacking Israel, then it might precipitate a world war.

February 6, 1958

Received a return call from the Ambassador of Switzerland in the morning. He was very keen to know what our Government's attitude was towards the demand made by certain nations such as Indonesia and the Latin American countries for an extension of the present limit of territorial waters. I said that since we were interested in fishing rights, most probably Malaya would like the present limit to stay put.

In the afternoon, I received a call from one Mr. Granlund, an insurance agent. I was shocked to hear him advising me not to tell the insurance doctor that I was suffering from a rheumatic heart, should I be asked about it in the course of medical examination. Needless to say that I rejected this preposterous suggestion. It just shows that one must not be too gullible when dealing with American businessmen.

In the evening, I attended a dinner given by Mr. & Mrs. De La Mare of the British Embassy. Eric Kocher was there and he mentioned the possibility of he and Robertson, Under-Secretary of State (Far Eastern Affairs) visiting Malaya for a couple of days after the SEATO meeting.[31] I said, I wished the visit would take place, particularly in view of the news I had received from Tunku and Dato' Razak and about which I was going to speak to him after lunch on Saturday.

De La Mare, after the dinner, asked my opinion about the Indonesian situation. I said that unless England and America helped the Masjumi and the moderate leaders to come to power, Indonesia would become Communist. In answer to another question, I said that Soekarno would fall on the winning side in Indonesia. He said that the U.K. and possibly America were waiting anxiously.[32]

I cannot help thinking how devoid of initiative the Western Powers are!

February 9, 1958

I invited Kocher, who is now Director of South-East Asian Affairs in the State Department, and his wife to lunch at the Embassy to discuss further

---

[31] Malaya never joined SEATO, the Southeast Asian Treaty Organisation, formed in the 1950s to battle communism in the region. Its members were the United States, the United Kingdom, France, Australia, Thailand, the Philippines, New Zealand, and Pakistan. Pakistan pulled out in 1973, and France in 1974. SEATO formally ended in 1977.

[32] Partai Majelis Syuro Muslimin Indonesia (Masyumi) was formed in 1945, and was the strongest Muslim and anti-communist party in Indonesia. It won the first Indonesian general elections in 1955, and its leader Burhanuddin Harahap became the country's first elected prime minister. The party was banned in 1960 by President Soekarno.

the subject of loans, which he sometime ago first brought to my attention on hearing from the American Ambassador in the Federation of Malaya. I told Kocher that I had written to Dato' Razak about it and had received his reply. It was to the effect that the Federation Government had applied for two specific loans for its Development Plan — one was for the Klang wharf extension and the other for [the] University Teaching Hospital site plan. Kocher said that he had heard further from his Ambassador that the Federation would apply for $200 million (Malayan) for kampong development and that the Prime Minister himself would come to negotiate the loan. The American Ambassador had been asked to discourage the Prime Minister from making the trip for this specific purpose, although the Americans would just love to have him here for a visit especially, if he were going to attend the next Session of United Nations. The reason is that the State Department did not think that the application for such a loan would be successful. Americans, according to Kocher, are hard-headed businessmen and Congress would only agree to give loans on sound economic basis.

I asked him whether Malaya could not qualify for grants or economic aid or even loans on military and political grounds and quoted the Emergency, as an example, of Malaya's effort to fight international Communism; and since the result of Emergency would affect the free world, would not America be interested in giving aid to Malaya?

Kocher said that military aid was given under mutual assistance agreement. Under the agreement, there is a condition for the establishment of United States Military Mission in the countries receiving aid. It is under this type of agreement that countries like Laos and Vietnam are receiving American Aid. It is thought unlikely that Malaya would like such a condition. Further the Americans do not like to act in countries, where United Kingdom is giving military help and in Malaya about 50 per cent of the total cost of the Emergency, both in men and money are borne by United Kingdom.

Kocher certainly thought that it would be unwise for the Prime Minister himself to come to United States of America for the specific object of securing a loan or a grant to be spent on projects not based on sound economic grounds. As for projects based on sound economic grounds, the avenue is the Development Loan Fund, which is almost exhausted.

February 10, 1958

Received a cable from External [Affairs] on the Government's agreement to the proposal by the International Tin Council to set up a "special fund". Discussed with [Richard] Coursen of the Tin Bureau, since he received a cable from the Chairman of the F.M.S. Chamber of Mines which stated among other things, to "liase" with me. A statement was issued to the Press, based on the cablegram received from External. Coursen also told me that United States steel manufacturers had brought to his attention the fact that Malaya, based on reliable enquiries made by their intelligence, was exporting quantities of tin beyond the quota allotted to her for the period by the International Tin Agreement. I told Coursen that if this were true, there must be an explanation, because I could not imagine that Malaya intentionally would wreck an agreement, which she took great pains to secure. Probably the explanation is that the tin which is being shipped now from Malaya was produced before the quota system was imposed. In any case, Coursen had cabled to the F.M.S. Chamber of Mines for an explanation.

February 11, 1958

I paid a call on the Polish Ambassador. He was recovering from a bad cold. He had served in England and Argentina. We talked a lot on Argentina. The Ambassador said they were the greatest meat-eaters and meat was cheap in Argentina. He asked about the Embassies we have opened up and was surprised that we had not particularly opened one in Japan. He was particularly interested in Japan and said she was a great nation. He was particularly glad that I called on him and remarked that it was a pity that modern diplomatic practice had almost dispensed with "calls".

We received a note from Coursen stating that our Press release on tin was well received and that the price had firmed and he attributed it to our Press release.

February 14, 1958

Attended a meeting of the Afro-Asian bloc presided over by Monsieur Mongi Slim, the Tunisian Ambassador to the USA, and Permanent

Representative to the United Nations. The subjects discussed were Algeria, Tunisia and West Irian.

ALGERIA. The representative of F.L.N., which is an organisation of Algerian nationalists, who was invited to the meeting said that the French way of observing the resolution passed by the last General Assembly of the UN, was to ask the Algerian nationalists to surrender their arms and stop fighting, whereas the nationalists interpreted the resolution to mean a ceasefire, without the Algerian nationalists being placed at a disadvantage as, for example, the surrender of arms. The Indonesian Ambassador told the meeting that the Indonesian Parliament had passed a resolution, which had been transmitted to the French Government, to the effect that it considered the execution of a girl Algerian nationalist, caught by the French, as an inhuman act. The representative of the F.L.N. stated that the President of France had stayed the execution and further added that the girl had told her French captors that if she were executed, it would be the end of freedom for France.

TUNISIA. Monsieur Mongi Slim said that in the area where the French had dropped her bombs, there were no Algerian nationalists. In fact, in that area, there was a team of Red Cross. The French used, among other weapons, 21 planes and the bombing killed 31 people and injured over a hundred. They were all Tunisians and practically there were no Algerians.

The Tunisian President, as a result of the bombing, took every precaution to protect the lives of French men and women. He was adamant that because of the bombing no French soldiers must be stationed in Tunisia, and he had arranged for the safe conduct of French soldiers to the harbour. His country is submitting the issue to the Security Council and, if vetoed by France, she would ask for an Emergency Session of the General Assembly, but Monsieur Mongi Slim hoped that this would not become necessary.

WEST IRIAN. The Indonesian Ambassador in his statement said much that is already common knowledge. He said that the problem which Indonesia is facing internally must be viewed separately from the question of West Irian.

As regards the question of West Irian, it was not true that the Dutch were expelled from Indonesia. What actually happened was that the Indonesian

Government had asked "unemployed Dutch aliens to leave the country". The Government had not nationalised Dutch industries, but had used the powers, which already existed before World War II, to take supervisory action over industries in times of Emergency. Indonesians had not closed the door for negotiation, but the Dutch had not taken the initiative. The Ambassador stressed the unity of Indonesians of whatever political flavour in this fight against the Dutch over West Irian.

As regards the internal problem, the rebels in Sumatra questioned the powers of the President to set up a Government without going through a formateur.[33] The Ambassador said that under the constitution, the President, in an Emergency, had powers to appoint a Cabinet. He further added that much of the trouble was caused by a lack of shipping which was vital to Indonesia which consisted of islands. The Dutch had the monopoly of shipping and when the trouble started, she diverted about 30 ships to Singapore. However, with the help of Japan and other countries, normal communication was restored.

ACTIONS TO BE TAKEN. There was considerable discussion as to the procedure to be adopted, i.e. whether a letter should be despatched to the Secretary-General or a Delegation should be appointed to meet the Secretary-General or whether both of these actions should be combined.

Then there was discussion as to whether all the three problems should be represented together. The Indonesian Ambassador was against including the question of West Irian because his country had made it clear that she herself would not take any further action in UN.

I intervened and said that in whatever form the representation was to be made, it was impossible to divorce completely the question of Algeria from that of Tunisia. The object of the UN resolution was to contain the question

---

[33] A rebellion in Sumatra had broken out in February 1958, and dissident politicians and militarists on the island formed the Pemerintah Revolusioner Republik Indonesia (PRRI, Revolutionary Government of the Republic of Indonesia). Officially, Malaya did not support the rebellion, but since cultural and commercial ties between Sumatra and the Malay Peninsula were intense, and also because the rebels were anti-communists, suspicions were strong in Jakarta that Malaya was helping the rebels in various ways.

of Algeria and since the French refusal to comply with the UN resolution had resulted in this incident in Tunisia, it was better to mention in the representation on Tunisia the relevant question of Algeria.

The Ambassador of Ceylon then produced a draft Press statement which, in general, expressed deep concern over the French assault on an independent country.

At this juncture, I had to leave to have lunch and to catch the plane to Washington. I gave specific instruction to Tunku Ja'afar, whom I had asked to take my place, to telephone to me in Washington the results of the meeting. Imagine my surprise and consternation when I received a telephone call in the Embassy on my return from Lim Taik Choon, the First Secretary, to the effect that he had received a phone call half an hour earlier from Tunku Ja'afar, who said that since he was going to a Cocktail, Lim was to tell me that Tunku Ja'afar had sent a cable to External reporting the results of the meeting.

It is unthinkable that a First Secretary should communicate to External on such an important subject without at least having the courtesy to show to the Permanent Representative the text of the cablegram before despatching it.

I am sending a cablegram in cipher to External reporting the matter.[34]

February 15, 1958

The New York Times carried the news that the Afro-Asian Group called on the Secretary-General to express deep concern over the deterioration of the situation in Algeria generally. The Committee consisted of the representatives of Indonesia, Tunisia, Ceylon, Ethiopia and Burma.

The same paper also announced that a meeting of the Security Council will be held on Tuesday, the 18th instant at 3.00 p.m. to discuss the Tunisian question.

---

[34] The embassy and mission had no coding system for communication with Kuala Lumpur, and they invented one, using Malay. Since communication was slow, the standard practice was: "if we don't hear from you after such and such a time, we will assume that you agree with our suggested lines of action". Such a situation meant that Dr Ismail made a lot of decisions on foreign affairs on the spot (Drifting c13).

No news from Tunku Ja'afar. I give up trying to "take this man under my wings".

February 16, 1958

I gave a buffet lunch to teachers from Malaya, who had been touring the United States on international teachers exchange programme. It was interesting to hear their views of the United States of America. All were of the opinion that much of the information which United States citizens have of Malaya was either erroneous or outdated. One teacher quoted how some Americans in one town which he visited looked upon Malaya as an undeveloped country, inhabited by people who live in houses built on stilts. These people gained this knowledge by reading an encyclopedia published in 1936. All were in agreement on the wonderful hospitality extended to them.

It had been snowing very hard; in fact, reports said it was the heaviest snowfall in 26 years. The teachers had to wade their way through the thick snow, but they said the Malayan food served to them more than compensated for their inconvenience.

February 17, 1958

The snow, which had fallen for the last $1^1/2$ days, lay thick on the ground. Newspapers carried news of people dying of cold, dislocation of public transport, motor cars stalling on the roads, offices and schools closed.

I had to cancel the dinner which I had arranged weeks before.

I managed to wade my way through the snow to get to the office station wagon (the Ambassador's car being marooned in the garage) parked a quarter of a mile away from the Embassy. I was driven to the State Department to keep an appointment with Robert Murphy, Deputy Under-Secretary for Foreign Affairs.

Mr. Murphy is a fairly oldish man, but his appearance belied his years. Although an extremely busy man he managed to appear relaxed. Although the conversation was general, he was deeply interested in the economy of Malaya and in our views on the Indonesian problem. In the former he asked questions on Tin, Rubber and our trade with Japan. In the latter, he was particularly interested to hear that culturally, and in language there were more similarities between the Malays and Sumatrans than between the Malays and the Javanese. I was particularly careful to remark that in the present quarrel in Indonesia we are not taking sides and we are even careful not to give the appearance that we are taking sides.

February 18, 1958

Snow is still on the ground and the temperature is still too low for the snow to melt.

The Minister[35] had just returned from attending a conference in London to prepare the agenda for the Commonwealth Conference on Economics to be held in Montreal on 15th September. Among the news he brought home was that of Dato' Nik Kamil's impending departure for Malaya to assume the office of Permanent Secretary to the Department of External Affairs. The Minister also remarked that in contrast to London our offices in Washington and New York were less in confusion.

The Charge d'Affaires of the Embassy of Hungary made a courtesy call. I was somewhat unhappy of this call, when I first heard it from the Special Assistant, Miss [Daisy] Yee; who is in charge of all my official and social engagements. I asked the First Secretary, Mr. Lim Taik Choon, who is in charge of Protocol in our Embassy, to inquire into this case. According to him, on the advice of the Dean of the Diplomatic Corps it would be impolite to refuse such a call.

The Charge' called in at 4 o'clock and stayed only for 15 minutes. He said that he had been Charge' for about two years, that is "since the unfortunate incident between my country and America, which resulted in the recall of our Ambassador". He asked questions on the number of our diplomatic missions abroad, particularly in Europe in which he included England and also on the economy of Malaya. I had no difficulties in answering to them. He said that Hungary, since World War II had embarked on industrialisation

---

[35] Economic minister at the embassy, Ismail Ali.

and today 60 per cent of her economy is based on industrial production. She has successfully competed in international markets for contracts on construction of power plants and on building dams. For example, in India she succeeded in winning contracts, "thanks to Mr. Nehru" on construction of hydroelectric plants; in Egypt a Hungarian firm is engaged on the construction of the Aswan Dam. Diplomatic Hungary has a unique relationship with Japan since the War days, which still is in existence. Hungary was under Fascist Germany, and in the War Japan was Germany's ally. Evidently, this relationship has not been severed or replaced. Hungary has also economic relations with Indonesia. She has no economic agreement with the United States of America, but she sells a number of industrial products to the United States of America, such as Expresso Coffee Machines, which she has been selling by the thousands. According to the Charge', with the United States of America economic agreement is not necessary.

He said that his economic minister will no doubt contact "your colleagues".

February 19, 1958

Last night I and my wife attended a dinner given by the Chiefs of Missions to the former Dean of Diplomatic Corps at the Statler Hotel. I would have enjoyed the dinner very much had it not been for an unfortunate incident, which occurred at the reception prior to the dinner.

Each guest was given a card on which was written the name of a lady, whom he was to escort to the dinner table. The name of the lady on my card was unknown to me. As the Ambassador of Israel was passing by I stopped him to make the enquiry. Imagine my surprise, when our conversation was interrupted by the Charge' d'Affaires of Syria, who had suddenly come up to lead me away to a group of Ambassadors from the Arab States, among whom was the Ambassador of Saudi Arabia. He then began to lecture to me in front of the group on the impropriety of my action in having indulged in social intercourse with the Ambassador of Israel. My attempt to explain that my having social contact with the Ambassador of Israel did not necessarily mean that I support Israel in her quarrel with the Arab States, was brushed aside. I was therefore compelled to write a memo to the Charge' this morning and a copy of it together with an explanatory letter was sent to Tunku.

At last night's dinner, I also heard from the Ambassador of Thailand that he was making representation to the Protocol Section of the State Department on the manner the invitation to the White House dinner was issued. According to the procedure adopted, Ambassadors were classified into "odds" and "evens" in order of seniority. The Ambassador of Thailand was in the "odds" and yet he was invited on the night when the "evens" were invited. This incident shows how important protocol can be at times, and yet practically no one among our foreign service personnel has any knowledge of protocol. Our First Secretary told me that whatever protocol he had learnt was gained during the period he had served in our Embassy in Washington.

February 21, 1958

Left with First Secretary [Lim Taik Choon] by plane for New Orleans in the State of Louisiana, on the first leg of our tour of Southern States of the United States of America.

We left Washington at 8.40 a.m. and arrived in New Orleans at 2 pm. We were booked in at St. Charles Hotel, where we were met by a representative of the International House. He had arranged for us to visit Shell oil refinery plant, which was situated about 25 miles out of New Orleans. At the refinery we were met by Mr. Harrison and Mr. Richards. After a short briefing on the history of the refinery, they took us on a tour of the plant.

The Shell Company in the United States of America is the sixth biggest of oil companies and its refinery near New Orleans is one of its largest. The Company, although it bears the name of Shell and a large share of its business is owned by the Royal Dutch Oil Company, which is a majority shareholder of Shell international, has its own independent management. The Company only caters for USA market and this particular refinery supplies the eastern board of USA. The crude oil comes mainly from the Company's own oil fields in the Gulf of Mexico. It buys but little from other oil-fields.

The plant is so streamlined and so well planned that we made our tour in Mr. Richards' car, without even stepping out of it. The refinery employed about 1,500 people, although we hardly saw any of them during our tour. It has quarters for its staff and schools for the employees' children.

February 21, 1958

We were met by Mr. Weekly of the Kaiser Aluminium Factory at our hotel. On arriving at the factory, we were shown the research laboratory, where the products of the factory were tested for its metal composition. Unfortunately, the machine was out of order and so we missed the demonstration. The research centre is, so to speak, outside the confines of the factory proper.

At the gate of the factory we were each issued with a pass by the security guard.

The factory is gigantic. It is very streamlined and all structure is of steel. The main portion is devoted to plants, which generate electricity. This factory is a reduction plant, in that aluminium bauxite is reduced by electrical supply to alumina. It requires 10 kilowatts of electricity to produce 1 lb. of alumina from 2 lbs. of aluminium bauxite. The alumina is produced in the form of "pigs", which is really a solid, wedge-shaped, block of metal, in the form of cylinders, and in sheets. From this factory these various forms of alumina are shipped to fabricating plants where they are made into all sorts of utensils.

After the tour we invited Mr. Weekly to a drink at the hotel, in the course of which we discussed the colour problem in the South. Mr. Weekly, who is a northerner but has a southerner as a wife was very sympathetic to the negroes. He had been to school and college with negroes and had admired their mental capacity. It was a shock for him that when he visited his hometown after a period of absence to see his negro friends working only as domestic servants, factory hands and other manual work, because they had been denied opportunities on account of their colour. His observation led him to the conclusion that this prejudice against the negroes in the South is based on fear. According to him, the negroes are more fertile, better craftsmen in the South and if given the opportunities may compete successfully against the white.

In the afternoon, we went to see horse racing. The track is beautifully laid out. It is sandy and in the centre is placed a beautiful garden, which we could not see at its best because of the heavy rain and the recent snow downfall, which, incidentally, occurred for the first time in the living memory of most New Orleans. The grand stand is not unlike those one sees in

Malaya. The latrines have distinct signs — White only. I went into one of them, but was not molested. Evidently, "coloured" in the South means negroes or those who could be mistaken for negroes. There were also negroes among the race-goers but not one of them entered into any of these latrines for "White only". Either they have a huge urinary bladder or they must have strained themselves, because the weather was cold and no one could possibly go through the whole afternoon without emptying his bladder.

February 24, 1958

Spent the afternoon on the river boat, cruising on the Mississippi along the harbour. Ships flying the flag of many countries were at anchor along the wharfs, some loading, some unloading cargoes. It was amusing to hear the commentator on the boat calling our country the Malaya States in the course of his description of the destinations to which these ships were going.

February 25, 1958

In the morning went by taxi to a mahogany factory. It was small and its business depended more on the quality rather than on quantity of its products.

Called on the acting Mayor with Mr. Gomez of International House, the Mayor having gone out of town. I was pleasantly surprised, when the Mayor presented a certificate and a gold key making me a free citizen of New Orleans.

My impression of New Orleans is that it is a city which has managed to retain traces of the influence of its past masters, especially the French. This is especially evident in that section of the city where old buildings of French architecture are not only preserved but in cases when they are demolished because of extreme old age, new buildings built in their places must conform with the old design.

The people of New Orleans retain the prejudices, which the Southerners have of the negroes. These prejudices are difficult to eradicate, because they are based on fear and emotion, totally devoid of reason. For example, one of the taxi drivers, who drove us, was asked by me why he disliked negroes. His reply was that he was not obliged to give his reasons. It was enough that he hated them and that they bred like flies. Eisenhower, according to him, lost his popularity, apart from the fact that employment was rising and recession came during his presidency, due to his sending Federal troops to Little Rock to enforce desegregation in school.

February 26, 1958

Our plane to Pensacola was delayed and we did not leave New Orleans until 1.30 p.m. and arrived in Pensacola at 4 pm. We were the guests of the Admiral. We were taken around to see the Naval Air Training School. Besides Americans, people from such countries as Iran and Pakistan came to Pensacola for training. We left Pensacola at 9 o'clock in the evening full of memories of the superb hospitality of the Admiral who even took the pain of giving a cocktail party in our honour. We arrived in Jacksonville amidst torrential rain at 1.30am local time.

February 27, 1958

In Jacksonville, we hired a "drive your own" car. We left Jacksonville at 11 o'clock in the morning travelling towards Melbourne, a town half way between Jacksonville and Miami. Our route took us through Daytona, famous for its long stretch of beach where many world motor-car speed records are made and broken. All along the way we passed scenery which is sub-tropical and made me nostalgic of Malaya.

February 28, 1958

We left Melbourne for Miami. We travelled along the Parkway for 300 miles without traffic lights and stopping. The Parkway passes through park land, which was monotonous in its scenery. American Parkways are wonderful to drive on, but the monotony and the speed with which you travel are conducive to accidents.

Miami, the world famous winter resort, is full of hotels and motels. Contrary to common belief, it is not exclusively for the rich. Of course, there are hotels like Eden Roch, Fontainbleau and the Americano, which charge fabulous rates, but on the other hand the motels are luxurious, very convenient for motorists, especially those with families and what is important, their rates are very reasonable.

Monday, March 3, 1958
Tuesday, March 4, 1958

Spent both days in New York office. Tunku Ja'afar brought to my attention a letter, dated some time in October, from the External Affairs, asking information on security arrangements in the office. I could not understand why he had allowed months to lapse before bringing it to my attention. I went to examine the strong room. To my surprise and consternation, he did not know how to work out the combination lock, nor did Lim, the Second Secretary, to whom Tunku Ja'afar entrusted everything connected with secrecy and security arrangements. He had drafted a reply to the questionnaire attached to the External Affairs letter and asked me to sign the letter. When I read that External Affairs letter instructed that the reply should be only routed through me, I told him to comply with the instruction. I have ceased to be angry with Tunku Ja'afar, because it would only affect my blood pressure. He seems impervious to correction.

In the evening I gave a talk to a graduate association of the New York University. The audience consisted mainly of teachers and my talk was confined mainly to a description of Malaya on such topics as the economic, the geography, and the constitution of the country. Besides myself, there were other speakers from the missions of Japan and Ghana.

Wednesday, March 5, 1958

Dinner at the Embassy in honour of Walter Robertson, Assistant Secretary of State, who was going to the S.E.A.T.O. meeting and later on to the Federation of Malaya, which latter visit he had to abandon because of medical advice. There were present also two Congressmen and their wives (Dr. Judd from the House of Representatives, and Senator Smith from the Senate) and Ambassador Khoman of Thailand and Madam Khoman.

There was some awkward moment prior to the dinner, because a problem on protocol suddenly cropped up. Mr. Robertson, being an Assistant Secretary, ranked below the Ambassador and the two Congressmen. According to protocol, the others should have been asked before invitations were issued to them whether they would waive their precedence in favour of Robertson. However, each of the people concerned was asked over the phone, and since they all knew Robertson well they readily agreed to waive their precedence in favour of him. This is another example why our foreign service officers must learn protocol before they are posted to our missions abroad.

Thursday, March 6, 1958

Went to the opening of the Flower Show as an invited guest, but there was no one to receive us. I am getting used to the way associations in America abuse their invited guests.

In the evening, I went to two Independent Day Celebrations — one at the Embassy of Cambodia and the other, Ghana, at Shoreham Hotel. Both were elaborate affairs. Ghana, especially, had invited no less than 700 guests and a special film unit from the United Nations to get "shots" of the reception. I cannot imagine either of these celebrations costing less than $2,000 American.

Friday, March 7, 1958

Had to get up very early in order to be "shot" by the United Nations Film Unit at the Embassy. The United Nations Film Unit is making a film of "a day in the life of the Ambassador of the Federation of Malaya".

In the afternoon at 4.30 pm, accompanied by the Minister and the First Secretary, went to the State Department to participate in the ceremony of signing the Agreements with the International Bank for Reconstruction and Development [IBRD] and the International Monetary Fund [IMF].

It was the first time I had an opportunity of talking to Mr. Dillon, Deputy Under-Secretary for Economic Affairs. He gave me the impression of quiet efficiency. In his address he particularly mentioned how pleased the American Government was to hear our Prime Minister's speech in which he advocated a charter for private enterprise in South-East Asia.

Monday, March 10, 1958

We went with Mr. and Mrs. George Weaver and the Minister and *isteri* [Ismail Ali and his wife Maimunah Latiff] to the opening of the American Ballet, after having an early dinner at the Embassy. George and his wife are very cultured negroes. He is an official of an American Labour Organisation called AFL-CIO.[36] He knows our Prime Minister very well.

He has promised to let me have a list of prominent labour leaders in America whom I can invite to the Embassy.

Thursday, March 13, 1958

Left with the Minister [Ismail] by 8 a.m. plane for Indianapolis, a midwestern town in the State of Indiana. Arrived at 9.20 a.m. local time, which is one hour behind Washington time.

We were met at the airport by Mr. Raredon, President-elect of Anderson College, Dr. Loh, a Chinese Doctor of Philosophy, who is an Associate Professor of Sociology at Anderson College and Dr. Ong, current President of the Malayan Students Association. From Indianapolis we drove in a car for about 45 miles to Anderson, our car being escorted by the State Police cars, which had their siren shrieking all the way, thereby drawing public attention to us.

After checking in at Anderson Hotel where we had a wash, we went to the Lions Club, where I gave a talk on Malaya. Lions Club is one of the "service" clubs in America and its activities are similar to those of Rotary. LIONS stands for Liberty Intelligence Our Nation's Salvation.[37] Just before lunch all those present had to stand up and pledged their loyalty to USA.

---

[36] The American Federation of Labor and Congress of Industrial Organizations, is the largest national trade union center in the USA.

[37] This should be "Liberty Intelligence Our Nation's Safety".

My speech was confined to a description of Malaya, how it achieved its Independence, its constitution, its economy and where it resembles USA. At question time I was asked whether we would join S.E.A.T.O., to which I replied that the mandate of the present Government was to secure Independence and, as we are a democratic country, the Prime Minister had stated that the question of S.E.A.T.O. will have to be decided by the people at the next election to be held towards the end of 1959. This particular question kept on cropping up wherever I made a speech. The next equally frequent question asked was the state of Emergency in Malaya, to which I invariably replied by quoting the Prime Minister's statement that he hoped by the grace of God to finish it on the First Anniversary of our Independence. Another popular question was the new relationship between the Federation of Malaya and Great Britain, such as how much control Great Britain still has over Malaya on the question of finance and defence. I replied that we are now a fully, sovereign nation and whatever ties there are between us and Great Britain are mutually agreed upon on terms of equality without in any way involving any sacrifice of sovereignty on our part; for example, we remain in the Commonwealth of our own free choice, we signed the Defence Agreement with Great Britain of our volition in order to safeguard our country against external attack, we remain in the sterling area for practical reasons.

After lunch with the Lions Club we were taken to see a public school, which is equivalent to a private school in England, a tour of the city and a visit to Anderson College. The city of Anderson, I am told, is a typical mid-western industrial city. It is the home of General Motors, the motor-car firm which produces such cars as Cadillac, Chevrolet, Buick and Oldsmobile. Practically all the people other than shopkeepers earn their livelihood at General Motors factories.

Anderson College is somewhat equivalent to a university college. It grants degrees in Arts, Theology and Science. It has an enrolment of 1,200 students and boasts of a lovely campus and fine buildings. One of its chief benefactors is Mr. Wilson, one time Secretary of Defence of USA and a director of General Motors. It takes in foreign students as far away as Egypt. The students body consists of persons of all ages, some are adolescents, others are married men and women who live in caravans, which are parked in the campus. A campus is an American word for college or university grounds.

In the evening after a dinner given by Dr. Loh, we went to a reception in the newly opened college library. Besides the governing students body, dignitaries of the city were invited. All the guests without exception were interested in Malaya and all were unanimous in congratulating Malaya on achieving Independence by peaceful means.

Friday, March 14, 1958

At 7.30 a.m. we went to a breakfast reception organised by the Mayor's Committee on United Nations. The reception had to be held at such an early hour because the members of the Committee were working men and had to be at work. They consisted of men and women who one often sees in many cities and who are interested in civic work. One woman asked about the status of women in Malaya and was surprised when told that they had as much freedom, if not more than women in America.

At 9 o'clock we went to Anderson College, where in front of students numbering several hundreds I gave the same talk as I did at the Lions Club. The students were just as enthusiastic as, if not more so than, the members of the Lions Club in asking questions. One student from Jamaica was especially interested in our defence agreement with Great Britain. He was labouring under the misunderstanding that our defence was still under the control of Great Britain. The students as a whole were very impressed with our democracy and democratic institutions.

We then went to see the Model United Nations in Session. Every year, for about the last 10 years, Anderson College has sponsored a Model United Nations Session. About 20 schools in Anderson sent delegates to this Session and each delegation was named after a member nation of the United Nations. I was introduced to the Delegation bearing the name of our country, who in turn introduced me to the President of the Assembly. I made a short speech wishing the Assembly success.

At lunch time I gave the speech for which I was specially invited to Anderson. The audience consisted of the student delegations to the Model United Nations Session, their friends and distinguished citizens of Anderson.

My speech was of half-hour duration and along the lines of speeches which I had previously made at the United Nations Assembly.

We left Anderson for Chicago at 4.30 p.m. via Indianapolis in Dr. Ong's car. When we arrived at Indianapolis, Dr. Ong, who is a resident at Indiana General Hospital, took us around the city. The city is big, its buildings are mainly painted grey to withstand the soot from the industrial plants; it boasts of several monuments. We stopped at the Students Union. It is a luxurious building and has a swimming pool, a cafeteria, shops selling cosmetics, cigarettes, etc.. According to Dr. Ong, the maintenance charges are so high that at present it is being used more by members of the public than students, who cannot afford the prices charged. We left Anderson for Chicago at 5.30 p.m. and arrived in Chicago at 10 o'clock.

Saturday, March 15, 1958

We stayed at Conrad Hilton Hotel in Chicago. This hotel is the largest in the world, surpassing in size the famous Waldorf Astoria of New York, which has accommodation for 1,200 guests and which incidentally is also owned by Hilton.

Chicago shatters the image which I have of it. I had imagined Chicago as a densely congested city, with disorderly traffic and the air filled with dust and grime. However, from the window of our suite we had a lovely view of Lake Michigan in the distance, with beautiful boulevards spread before our eyes. Our tour of the city first took us to the suburb of Evanston. Here lives the well-to-do. The houses are varied in architecture and the beaches are strewn with yacht clubs and bathing facilities. We were told that the beaches are privately owned and one has to get a season ticket to be able to swim along the beaches.

In the evening I gave a dinner to the President and Committee members of the Malayan Students Association. This august body is called the Cabinet. During dinner they were especially interested to hear my views on American degrees. I told them that I had read the memorandum, which their Association had sent to the Federation Government. In general, I personally agree that American degrees should be recognised and that I shall make my recommendations accordingly. I also reminded them that the Federation had been independent only for the last 6 months and what with the shortage of staff and the number of matters to attend to, the Government could not possibly deal with their petition faster than it is doing now. The Government had set up a Committee to investigate into and make recommendations on American degrees. The Committee will undoubtedly take some time in its task. I was told by them that quite a number of Malayans who have American degrees in Engineering and Medicine are anxiously waiting. They wanted to go home and render their services to the country either in Government service or in industry, but they could not do so because their degrees are not recognised; on the other hand, they have been given tempting offers to join American firms, which if they accept would make them American citizens in the long run, and this latter prospect they are not very keen to do. They are Malayans and they want to render their services to Independent Malaya. I was moved by their loyalty. I told them that for those who had qualified and were prevented from going home because they would not be allowed to practise, I would be prepared to examine their cases individually and make my recommendations to the Government.

After talking to the "Cabinet" members of the Malayan Students Association, my conclusion is that the problems facing American degrees as far as Malaya is concerned can be divided into the following categories:

(1) Recognition of Degrees;
(2) Registration of Degrees;
(3) Employment in Government Service.

Recognition of American Degrees.
Recognition of degrees is usually accorded as between one university and another, and it is usually reciprocal.

Registration of Degrees.
This is done by a body set up by the Government of a country on a law passed by Parliament. Members of the profession concerned are invariably represented on the body. The registration body, unless there are reasons to the contrary, always registers degrees which are recognised by the university or universities in the country. It can be empowered to register degrees that are

not "recognised" but which have attained a standard of proficiency. It may grant exemption from registration to meet special needs. It may grant registration for a special purpose.

Employment in Government Service.
Government can employ persons with degrees which are not "recognised" and may ask the registration body to register them for that specific purpose, and if the existing law does not provide for it can amend the law.

Since the Federation is short of men with the necessary qualifications, the Government must discard the policy, introduced during the time when it was a colony, of registering only British degrees and adopt a new policy of recognising foreign degrees. The Government is now about to employ German doctors, who are not Federation citizens and whose degrees are not recognised and registrable under present laws. What is more logical than to do the same for its nationals? A further argument for recognising and registering American degrees is that America is easily the most industrialised country and leads the world in many branches of science and it is also a country where competition is very strong and therefore it is inconceivable that an American with an inferior degree can earn a livelihood in America. Unfortunately, false propaganda abroad has earned a bad reputation for American degrees.

After dinner we went to International House to meet the other Malayan students, one of whom had travelled 400 miles to attend the gathering. I was asked to give an impromptu speech. I talked to them of the history of our Independence movement and the new Constitution. I emphasised the need of racial harmony in order to build a united nation; the special position of the Malays, which was unanimously accepted by the non-Malays, because it was realised that equal opportunities for all in Malaya could only be practised if all were appropriately handicapped;[38] the danger of unscrupulous politicians

---

[38] Ismail's consistent view on equal opportunities, which he retained until his death in 1973, was that affirmative action should be conceived as a golf handicap system, where the weaker party is given an advantage in order that he or she could be allowed on the course, as it were. This use of the term "handicap" is sometimes misunderstood in general discussions to mean equality through hindering the stronger party.

making use of racial prejudices to gain power; the importance of leadership by all educated men of all races in Malaya, especially those who were fortunate enough to have their education abroad, in promoting racial harmony. I also mentioned of the talk, which I had had earlier with their "Cabinet" on the question of American degrees.

I was asked several questions on much the same lines as those I had encountered on this tour, but the question which seemed of particular interest to them, as was to be expected, was the question of American degrees. I was very much impressed with the students. They appeared to be hard-working, to have initiative and very loyal to Malaya. They did not give me the impression of being Leftists as the students I had met in Malaya Hall. The thing that moved me was their loyalty and their pride in our Independence. All this, coming from students, who are all Chinese, augurs well for the future of Malaya.

Sunday, March 16, 1958

Spent the whole day sight-seeing. We first went to Skids Row. This is a street infested with incurable drunkards. They spend the whole day either drinking or begging. Then we went to the slums. The buildings here are dilapidated and the rooms are divided into cubicles where the inhabitants sleep covered with newspapers as blankets. The majority of these people are negroes.

Chicago has three methods of travel — by overhead railway, on roads and by subways. In one street, where there is this overhead railway, we noticed that the windows of the shops were barricaded with steel windows. We were told this was a protection against gangsters.

Monday, March 17, 1958

We arrived in Akron the previous night by plane from Chicago and were met by Mr. Klippert of Goodyear and Mrs. Klippert. We stayed at the Mayflower. In the morning at 9 o'clock we were driven in one of Goodyear's limousines to its office, where Mr. Klippert had arranged for us to tour the tyre-manufacturing section of Goodyear factories. In the course of the tour, which took one hour to complete, I was struck by the fact that large quantities of natural rubber are still used in tyre manufacturing. The heavy tyres such as those used in trucks, tractors, etc., are all made of natural rubber. Then we went to Goodyear foam-rubber plant. This is a new plant and designed in such a way as to give plenty of room for workers. Foam latex is poured at one end and after going through a series of machines, all pointing in one direction, the finished product is delivered at the other end.

We had luncheon with Mr. Thomas, who is the President of Goodyear and his top executives. Here, as in other places where we met rubber manufacturers in the course of our tour, the popular questions were centred on:

(1) our rubber production, and replanting programme;
(2) the Communist problem in Malaya;
(3) the state of labour;
(4) the attitude of the Federation Government in the present trouble in Indonesia.

It later transpired that all these questions were asked in order to predict whether the supply of natural rubber from Malaya is secure or not, and whether the price of natural rubber is going to soar or not. These two factors are very important in determining whether existing synthetic plants should be expanded or not and whether new plants to manufacture a new type of synthetic rubber, which has all the qualities of natural, should be built or not. I am convinced by these rubber manufacturers when they said that the future of natural rubber is very bright, for the following reasons:

(1) When the Government handed new synthetic plants to private enterprises it stipulated, in accordance with anti-Trust laws, that the prices of synthetic must not be fixed, in order not to victimise the small rubber manufacturers. As a result, the companies operating synthetic plants are selling it at very much the same price as when synthetic plants were in the hands of the Government.
(2) Future trends of wages and steel are going up in America.

(3) Existing synthetic plants are not suitable for the manufacture of newer types of synthetic.

(4) World demand for both natural and synthetic is steadily increasing.

However, this bright prospect of natural is conditional on natural rubber being produced in sufficient quantities to meet increasing demands and at prices competitive with synthetic.

After luncheon we went to see the plants belonging to Goodrich. We were taken to see Mr. Collyer, Chairman and Chief Executive and Mr. Keener, the President, who were both leaving for New York. Mr. Collyer was formerly with Dunlop and is reputed to be unpopular in South East Asia for his forthright statements on speculation of natural rubber. However, I found him personally a nice man. He congratulated our Government on the stability of our country and asked pertinent questions on natural rubber.

We were taken to see that section of Goodrich Company which concentrated on the manufacture of rubber goods of various kinds for the use of other industries. For example, the factory manufactures all types of belting and rubber parts for motor-cars.

In the evening, we were the guests of Mr. Ormsby, President of the Rubber Manufacturers Association, who was responsible for the excellent arrangements of our tour of Akron rubber world. Present at the dinner were the big bosses of rubber world, including Mr. Firestone, one of the sons of the founder of Firestone Rubber Company. It was a lovely dinner, remarkable for its informality and memorable for its food. I was asked to give a speech, in which I described Malaya's effort to modernise its rubber plantations, the Government's policy of attracting private capital, with special emphasis on Tunku's speech at E.C.A.F.E. on the subject, and I also made a personal appeal for American capital to go to Malaya, because I considered American capitalism as "modern capitalism" which brings benefits not only to the investors but also to labour and the country. I was told afterwards that my frank statement was very welcome.

Tuesday, March 18, 1958

We started the day by going through Firestone research laboratory. The Director, Mr. Staveley, had done research in Sumatra in the twenties. He had more than 100 scientists working under him. We were shown all types of research involving both natural and synthetic, with a bias on synthetic. We were shown a new type of synthetic called "coral" rubber, which, we were told, has all the qualities of natural rubber. For it to be commercially produced, a new type of synthetic plant has to be built. As yet, there is no indication that it is going to be built.[39]

The highlight of the tour, as far as I was concerned, was when we were taken through the synthetic plant of Firestone. It is worth comparing the relative merits and demerits of both this synthetic plant of Firestone and its 90,000 acres of rubber plantation in Liberia. Both produce the same amount of rubber, but the synthetic plant requires only limited space, while the plantation needs 90,000 acres of land; Firestone rubber plantation definitely employs more labour than its synthetic plant, but the cost of labour is higher in America than in Liberia and the capital cost of the synthetic plant is definitely greater than that of its rubber plantation; maintenance cost of its synthetic plant is definitely higher than that of its rubber plantation. These are but some of the comparisons. My impression is that this particular plant is already antiquated and whether it will be modernised and a new plant built will depend on the price of natural as compared to that of synthetic.

As if to take away the bitter taste of synthetic from our mouth, we were shown a film of Firestone rubber plantation in Liberia. Firestone is given a big land concession and we saw how big American capital brought development to the country in which it was invested. There were modern schools, modern hospitals with research centres, and good living accommodation for the workers.

At luncheon, I sat next to Mr. Firestone. He was very interested to hear my talk the previous night. He himself is hardworking and very popular with his staff.

After lunch we talked with Mr. Waugh, who is in charge of Firestone investment in foreign countries. The account of the talk is already elaborated

---

[39] The Bridgestone-Firestone's research center Internet homepage still boasts of its invention of coral rubber; "the first synthetic polyisoprene rubber, and the ensuing research that led to the company's entrance into commercial production of solution elastomers": <http://www.bridgestone-firestone.com/news/newsarchive_2004.asp?id=2004/040819a>.

in our official report to the Minister of External Affairs. What struck me most were two things. One is that foreign investment looks on the stability of both the Government of the country and the country itself, the other is the international economic standing of the country.

Just before we left for Washington in the private plane, owned by Goodyear, I gave a press interview. The main theme was our effort to streamline our industry and to attract foreign capital and in the latter case, I gave the reporters a copy of our Prime Minister's speech at E.C.A.F.E..

Thursday, March 20, 1958

Although it was damp and the roads were blocked, I and my wife went to the reception at the Tunisian Embassy. The Embassy is an impressive, white building situated on a hill. The interior is tastefully decorated and on the floors were strewn expensive Persian carpets. The Ambassador is a bachelor and he looked lonely as he stood alone to receive the continuous line of visitors. Protocol in Washington decrees that in official functions, the host and hostess must be at the receiving line of guests from the time the function begins until it ends.

Friday, March 21, 1958

In the morning, I received a return call from the Ambassador of Japan. As usual, the talk was on economics. He was very impressed to hear that our balance of trade is always in our favour. He hopes that trade with Japan will continue to prosper. He was very pleased to hear that we had bought buildings for our Embassy in Japan and that Suleiman [Ismail's elder brother] was being sent by the Prime Minister to Japan to recruit staff and supervise the furnishing. He asked whether there was a possibility of Khir Johari, whom he met at an E.C.A.F.E. Conference in India, being sent as Ambassador, because he said Khir expressed the hope that he would be the Federation's first Ambassador to Japan. I told him that it was very unlikely as Khir was doing good work as Minister of Education.

In the evening, I entertained the top executives from World Bank, Import-Export Bank, I.F.C. and I.M.F. and Regional Director of I.C.A. to dinner.[40] Again there was a slip on Protocol. Mrs. Garner, the mother of Mr. Garner, President of I.F.C. was the oldest lady and should have precedence over all other ladies.

I told Mr. Moyer, the Regional Director of I.C.A., in answer to his question on our economy, that our country is finding difficulty in financing our budget and Development Plan without a Central Bank. He said that the first thing Vietnam did when it became independent was to establish a Central Bank with American help. Before that, Vietnam was wholly dependent on commercial banks. He also said that in Vietnam the French was realistic and was helping the Vietnamese to develop the economy of their country. This, he said, was in contrast to the Dutch, who, the Indonesians said, had never been reconciled with Indonesian independence.

Saturday, March 22, 1958

Went to lunch at the New Zealand Embassy to bid farewell to the Ambassador of Ceylon. It was a stag lunch. I met for the first time the new Australian Ambassador, Mr. Beale, and also Mr. Allison, who was recently the American Ambassador to Indonesia. Mr. Allison said that he saw a great deal of sense in Indonesia.

---

[40] The World Bank and the IMF were formed in Bretton Woods in July 1944, as part of the Allied Powers' efforts to establish post-war commercial and financial ties among industrial nations. The former consists of the International Bank for Reconstruction and Development (IBRD) and the International Development Association (IDA), with the aim of providing "low-interest loans, interest-free credit and grants to developing countries for education, health, infrastructure, communications and many other purposes". The IMF is geared towards stabilizing the international monetary system and to monitor world currencies. The Investment Finance Corporation (IFC) was formed in 1956 within the World Bank to work with private investors and invest in commercial enterprises in developing countries. The Import-Export Bank of the United States is a government-owned organization created in 1934 to provide guarantees of working capital loans for US exporters, guarantees loan repayments and makes loans to foreign purchases of US goods and services. The International Co-operative Alliance (ICA) is a non-governmental organization founded in 1895 by Christian Socialists.

Sunday, March 23, 1958

Gave a luncheon party to bid farewell to the Ambassador of Ceylon at the Embassy. Among the guests was Mr. Gunasekara. He is a Ceylonese and serves as alternate member on the executive board of I.B.R.D. and I.M.F.. He was keen to find out which country the Federation of Malaya would select to represent her on these bodies. I told him as yet I was very ignorant of the working of these bodies, although I had signed on behalf of the Federation agreements making us a member. Later on Ismail [Ali] told me that we had been allocated 500 votes by these bodies, much more so than many other members. It means that our voting strength is very considerable. According to Ismail also members serving as executives on I.B.R.D. and I.M.F. are chosen from "groups", each "group" comprises of several countries. These executive members once they are elected are paid remuneration by the bodies, and the amount is about $1,200 (U.S.)! No wonder, Mr. Gunasekara was very interested.

Ismail is investigating into the matter and will report to our Government.

Monday, March 24, 1958

Mr. Thackera, the Representative of Chase Manhattan Bank in Washington invited me and my wife to dinner at his house. The Thackeras live in a typical middle class house. The Americans call this type of house the "split" because one half of the house which is built on a higher level has only one storey, whereas the other half has a double storey.

Among the guests was Mr. Jacobson, Vice-Chairman of Chase Manhattan Bank in charge of the Bank's Far Eastern Affairs. He had just returned from a visit of the Far East with the Chairman. Mr. Jacobson said that he and the Chairman were very grateful to the Prime Minister and his colleagues for the royal reception accorded to them. Jacobson was very impressed with Malaya and was very impressed with the strength of Malaya's economy. When he mentioned that he had had a talk with our Adviser on Central Bank, I asked him when the Central Bank would be established. He disappointingly said that his impression was that it would be about 2 years. He also said that before his visit he had the impression that it would be established in about

6 months' time. Therefore, he said, there would be no business with Malaya for sometime. He appeared disappointed. When I asked him why it should take such a long time, he shrugged his shoulders and said "I don't know. There are so many types of central banks all over the world and you could choose anyone of them. It shouldn't take long to start a central bank." When I told him that Vietnam started a central bank very soon after Independence, he said that even Laos is having one and neither of these countries has such a strong and stable administration as Malaya.

I am really disappointed to hear of this delay in establishing a central bank. It is two years since the Report on Central Bank was discussed and yet the Bank itself is still a far away prospect. Central Bank is one of the attributes of Independence. Until a central bank is established we are not independent financially, and it is idle to talk of attracting foreign capital other than capital from Commonwealth countries. Americans, whom I have met, are chary of doing business unless we are financially independent of U.K..

Thursday, March 27, 1958

Left for New York in the official car. There has lately been a series of aeroplane accidents. The first one involved the plane carrying the film producer Mike Todd; the second one a military plane, the third one a Braniff plane, and in both cases a number of lives were lost; and in the fourth one a passenger plane had its wheels jammed, and after circling for hours above Washington airport managed to make a crash landing. I believe accidents, like trees bearing fruits, occur in seasons. I will go to New York in the car until the "season" is over.

My first appointment in New York was a luncheon party given by the Council of Islamic Affairs at Pierre Hotel. I had been a guest of honour at a luncheon given by the same organisation when the United Nations was having its twelfth session at the end of last year, and on that occasion I gave a talk on our country. On this occasion, the guest of honour was the Chief of General Staff of the United States Army, who unfortunately was unable to attend. His speech was read by his representative. The theme of the speech was the role of the Air Force in peacetime. It was a straight-forward speech, mainly descriptive and touched on nothing controversial. I sat in between the Permanent Representative of Lebanon and the editor, Mr. Armstrong, of the magazine "Foreign Affairs". Before the luncheon began, I had an interesting conversation with Mr. Esin, the Permanent Representative of Turkey to the United Nations. His view of the recent political change in Saudi Arabia, in which the King transferred much of his powers to his brother, Crown Prince Faisal, is that it is a manoeuvre to ease tension with Egypt rather than a quarrel between the two brothers, or the press report that Saudi Arabia was giving way to Egyptian pressure.

I have always admired Mr. Esin for his calmness and the able manner he represents his country at the United Nations. He has a charming wife. We parted with Mr. Esin expressing the wish of visiting the Federation of Malaya soon, to which I replied that we would be glad to receive him.

Friday, March 28, 1958

I spent the afternoon of the previous day and this morning at our New York Office. Miss Khoo, the Personal Assistant, who was working with me in the Ministry of Commerce and Industry at Kuala Lumpur and a very efficient worker, brought in the confidential and secret files. There were cablegrams sent in code to External Affairs on political matters without prior consultation with me or, if this was impossible, at least to send me simultaneously as the cablegrams were sent, a copy of it. I also found that it was the practice to send a copy of coded cablegram, if a copy was sent to Washington, in decoded form under confidential cover. I told Miss Khoo in future to send a copy of the coded message to Washington, where Mr. Kok can decode it. This will ensure complete secrecy.

I checked the duties of the office workers and how they perform them, and found them satisfactory.

In the afternoon, I had luncheon with Mr. McCoy of the Standard Vacuum Oil Company and his regional manager in Singapore Mr. White. Mr. McCoy was interested in trying to get a Malay to work with his Company. The job will be to inform the Government of the Federation of Malaya and its people what Standard Vacuum Oil Company stands for, and also in turn to inform the Company what the Federation of Malaya

Government and its people think of the Company and the things the Company should do to help the country and her people. The type of person suitable for the job is a man of about 30 to 40 years of age, although if no person within this age range is available a man in his early forties is suitable. The Company is not anxious to get an elderly man who can only put in a few years of service. A university qualification would be desirable, but not indispensable. The prospective candidate must have a flair for public relations work and able to discuss with the high executives of the Company, Government officers and Ministers on matters which affect the Company. A successful candidate will be sent to USA for six months to work in the Company Headquarters. Of course, the services of the successful candidate can be terminated by either side.

It seems to me this is an ideal job for an ambitious Malay with intelligence and who possesses the necessary qualifications.

Monday, March 31, 1958

Went to a cocktail party given by the British Ambassador in honour of British Consuls-General in America. Met a couple, whose names I can't remember (I am not good at all in remembering names), but the man was Head of Chancery of the Commissioner-General's Office in Singapore at the time when Malcolm MacDonald was the Commissioner-General. He was surprised to hear that Communist terrorism in Malaya was no longer a threat to our constituted Government. I also met the British Consul-General at San Francisco. He served in Germany during the period of German economic recovery. When I said that German economic recovery was really phenomenal, he agreed with some qualifications such as: Germany did it with the help of American and British loans, to which I replied Great Britain also had a share of American loans, but her recovery was not as phenomenal as Germany's; Germany had not to spend money on armaments.

Wednesday, April 2, 1958

Arrived in New York at 12.30 p.m., but my room was not ready.

I went to attend a meeting of the Association for Asian Studies. The meeting took the form of a series of meetings, at each one of which a specific subject was discussed. I went to attend the one discussing Problems on India's Economic Development. It was called the Specialist Session because in contrast to sessions which are not listed Specialist, it has no other items on the agenda. The Chairman read his paper, in which he described and criticised simultaneously India's Second Five Year Plan. When he had finished, the subject was thrown open for discussion. It is hard to record down everything that was discussed. My impression is that India attempted to carry out her Second Five Year Plan using both private and State enterprises and the aim is to create a mixed economy of large and small industries linked to the cottage industries. To achieve this, various agencies were set up. In some cases subsidies were given, in others loans of varying interest rates were given, but in none was there a complete "hand-out". It is interesting to note that the States do not live up to the expectation of the Central Government in raising taxes to finance their share of the Plan. The local politicians, who although belonging to the same party — Congress Party — are looking after their own interests, particularly their popularity with the electorate. This sounds a familiar ring to me.

At 3.30 p.m. I went to New York Office to do some work.

Thursday, April 3, 1958

In the morning I went again to the meeting of the Association for Asian Studies to discuss Political Developments in South East Asia. Unlike the meeting of the previous one which I had attended, this meeting attempted to discuss no less than four items, and one of them was "Recent Constitutional Changes in Malaya".

The speaker on this subject on Malaya was Mr. Norman Palmer of the University of Maryland. I met Mr. Palmer in Kuala Lumpur in 1953. He was then holding a Cornell scholarship and had come to Malaya to do research on the politics of Malaya, for which on his return to America he was awarded a Doctorate. I was then a nominated Minister of Natural Resources. He had come to see me to ask questions on U.M.N.O. and M.C.A..[41]

---

[41] Ismail's correct title was Member of Natural Resources. The United Malays National Organisation and the Malayan Chinese Association were the two major parties in Malaya's ruling Alliance.

Mr. Palmer's presentation of his subject was disappointing. He opened it with a very rough skeleton sketch of the Constitution. He then began to give his views on why such a constitution was drafted and accepted and what conditions would result from such a constitution. On the first issue, he said that the Constitution was drafted to ensure the continued existence of British economic interests in Malaya, to preserve British interests in the strategic position of Malaya, to concentrate powers in the hands of a few. On the second issue, he said that the Constitution would perpetuate communalism, and would probably create political troubles in Malaya. None of these views was supported by a quotation or a reference to the Constitution. I found it hard to believe that a man who had earned his Doctorate on his research on the politics of Malaya could deliver such an incoherent and irrelevant speech. If it had come from a Britisher, one could well understand the reason for it. But for an American holding a responsible position in an American university [this] can but reflect the standard of some American universities.

I did not bother to stop for the discussion. It would take another speech from me to correct him. Evidently, since he left Malaya in 1954, his knowledge of Malayan politics gained first hand must be limited only up to that time. He must be totally ignorant of the most crucial and formative period for Malayan politics — the period [from] 1954 to 1955.

I spent the rest of the morning and the afternoon in the office.

In the afternoon Prince Aly Khan, the Pakistan Permanent Representative to the United Nations, called in at the office. I had not seen or met him before. I was impressed by his easy manner, informality, his ability to give his whole attention to a particular person, and his quickness to respond to his observation.

Monday, April 7, 1958

I gave a talk to the English-Speaking Union at Sulgrave Club. The Club is housed in one of those buildings which were once the houses of the rich in Washington. In fact, most embassies and clubs in Washington are housed in this type of buildings. The audience consisted mainly of old ladies of means, whose pastime is to broaden their knowledge of the world by attending "talks", punctuated by occasional trips abroad to places which have aroused their interests as a result of these "talks".

The subject of my talk was Malaya. I knew that I had had an attentive audience when question time came. Many and varied were the questions asked, ranging from the number of shipping lines which call at Singapore to the fate of the Communist terrorists in Malaya.

Tuesday, April 8, 1958

I gave a talk to the Far Eastern Luncheon Group consisting of men from the Pentagon, the USA equivalent of Ministry of Defence, and officials from the State Department. My talk was on Malaya's Development Plan. The questions asked were very searching, as was expected of an audience consisting of men well acquainted with the economies of South East Asia.

In the evening I went to dinner at the Burmese Ambassador's residence in honour of the Indian Ambassador's departure for India.[42] After dinner, discussion drifted to the subject of education in Burma. The Ambassador, who was one of the leaders of Burma's Independence movement, said that he was the man responsible for free education in Burma from primary grade to university. He said that he now regretted having done it, because the financial burden is too much for Burma's economy. The question, he said, was how to withdraw the policy, which he admitted was drawn up at the full flush of Independence, more emotional than realistic, and passed over the opposition of his colleagues, who were much younger than himself, in a cabinet consisting of all young men. However, he was full of praise of the co-operative spirit of the villagers, who provided the labour to build schools out of the building materials provided by the Government. This spirit and co-operation were also displayed whenever roads had to be built in the villages.

The most difficult problem was one of maintenance. This, the Government could not persuade the villagers to do. Coming back to the

---

[42] The Burmese ambassador was U Win.

problem of education, the Ambassador said that schools were easy to construct, because they were of simple construction and made of wood, which was readily available in the villages. The problem of teachers was not easily solved, and as a result of this the standard of education deteriorated.

At the dinner I also met Mr. and Mrs. Booker of the Australian Embassy. Mr. Booker knows Lim, our First Secretary at the Embassy, very well, as he lectured to the first batch of foreign service trainees from Malaya to which Lim belonged. Mr. Booker admitted that he did [not] know on what to lecture to the students, as the training scheme was set up for the benefit of Malayan trainees. He personally believed that the only way to learn foreign service was to serve in an embassy or in the foreign office. However, he admitted that since then the training had improved.

Wednesday, April 9, 1958

Went to New York in the car. Spent part of the morning and the whole afternoon in the office. Despatched a cable to External urging the necessity of receiving the Instruments for W.H.O. if Malaya were to attend a meeting of that body on May 18.

Thursday, April 10, 1958

Spent the morning in the New York Office. There was very little to do, and this is in marked contrast to Tunku Ja'afar's usual complaint that he was tied to routine work.

Attended the luncheon at Waldorf Astoria, given in honour of Dag Hammerskjöld, Secretary-General of the United Nations, on his fifth anniversary. The luncheon was attended by more than 700 persons. What impressed me most was the list of sponsors of the function, which composed of businessmen from all branches of American industry. This spirit of public spiritedness among businessmen, who come forward to sponsor functions which yield no personal profit or benefit, is typically American.

The Secretary-General lives up to his reputation of a quiet, modest, brilliant, efficient, man when he gave his speech.

Friday, April 11, 1958
Saturday, April 12, 1958

Arrived in Philadelphia from New York to attend a conference of the American Academy of Political and Social Science, on South East Asia, All the speakers, in contrast to those at the conference of Asian Studies, gave illuminating, informative and interesting addresses. The ones which impressed me most were given by Mr. Warburg, an American multi-millionaire, author of several books on politics; U Thant, Burma's Permanent Representative to the United Nations; and Ambassador [G.L.] Mehta of India. I did not agree with Mr. Warburg's criticism of American foreign policy, because what he said might be true theoretically but impossible in practice; his advocacy that Communist China should not be admitted to the United Nations, but I could not help being impressed by the clarity of his thinking and oratory. U Thant gave a controversial speech advocating friendly relations with Communist Russia on the strength of his belief that Communist Russia had no aggressive attention, and admission of Communist China to the United Nations. It was unfortunate that his speech sounded as if he was espousing the Communist cause, and this caused a "walk-out" by the pro-Kuomintang delegates, who are all Chinese. However, this "walk-out" made the audience more sympathetic to U Thant because although it did not agree with his views it did not want to deny him the right to express it. Here in America, as is illustrated in the instance I have just described, the right of free speech is vigorously upheld. The audience may violently disagree with the views of the speaker, but it will defend to the utmost his right to say it. Ambassador Mehta, as a contrast, gave a brilliant speech on nationalism in South East Asia in which, quoting his country as an example, he gave the colonial powers their dues in developing the countries which they had colonised, but he also mentioned that the help which former, underdeveloped colonies were asking of the West was not begging, but rather a right, because the prosperity of the West was built on the exploitation of the natural wealth of the East in the past.

Monday, April 14, 1958

Received a return call from Ambassador Beale of Australia.

Tuesday, April 15, 1958

Received a return call from the Ambassador of Netherlands. He was of the opinion that it would be only a matter of short time before the rebellion in Sumatra was quelled, but he expressed the hope that Sukarno would be more generous after this and give the "islands" autonomy. He asked my opinion whether America should recognise Communist China as his country had done on the principle that recognition does not mean approval. I said that I personally think that what is possible for medium and small powers to do, might not be in the interests of all non-Communist nations for the U.S.A to do, because while there are still two giants to defend the two ideologies, medium and small powers can practise free foreign policies. In the case of Malaya, it is certainly not in her interest for U.S.A. to recognise Communist China. So long as Communist China is "illegal", so long will our efforts to finish off the Emergency be made easier. When asked why we did not recognise either "China", I said that by doing so we have a great chance of avoiding ideological conflicts taking place on our soil and also giving the Chinese in Malaya the best chance of being loyal to Malaya.

Thursday, April 17, 1958
Friday, April 18, 1958

Both days were spent in Milwaukee, a mid-west industrial city on the shore of Lake Michigan in the State of Wisconsin. The Department of Asian Studies of the Marquette University in Milwaukee sponsored a two-day conference on South-East Asia countries. Among those who came as delegates were businessmen from such big international firms as Allis Chalmers; officials from the State Department who were concerned with this region and from the Department of Commerce; representatives of World Bank, International Monetary Fund, Federal Reserve Bank, United Nations and economists from Harvard University. I and the Ambassador of Thailand were invited as guest speakers. My subject was "A new nation outlook on American capital" and the Thai Ambassador's was "Foreign Investment in Thailand".

In my speech I outlined our Development Plan and the Federation's attempt to orientate its economy from a colonial one to that befitting an independent nation. At question time there were many questions asked, designed mainly to get answers, which clarified and elaborated the points I had made in my speech.

The other speeches were on the economic problems of Thailand, Burma, South Vietnam, Cambodia, Laos, Indonesia and Philippines. The subjects around which the discussion, following the speeches, was concentrated were (1) Industrialisation in the Region; (2) The Remission of Capital and Profits; (3) Diversification of Economy.

(1) Industrialisation in the Region.
It was the consensus of opinion that only industrialisation could secure economic prosperity in the region. Such countries as Australia and New Zealand, commonly known as primary producers, only have a small proportion of their population engaged in agriculture — in New Zealand the proportion is only 25 per cent.

(2) Remission of Capital and Profits.
A great deal of light was thrown on this problem by the representative of Allis Chalmers, a firm which manufactures such equipment as tractors and which operates outside USA in such sterling area countries as Australia. According to this representative, American investment in countries outside the Dollar Areas must be a long-term one. The investors must be prepared to reinvest its profits in the country in which it operates or, failing which, it must invest it in another country outside the Dollar Areas. When he was asked whether the shareholders could be content with no return of their investments, he replied that in the case of his company the mere fact that it was operating outside the country acted as stimulus, which increased the sales of its products in America. This resulted in large volume of profits to shareholders. The general conclusion on this problem was that American investors must make sure that before investing in these countries they get assurance that sufficient dollars will be available for remission of profits and capital if necessary.

(3) Diversification of Economy.

The general conclusion on this problem was somewhat qualified. It was conceded that diversification as a means to establish a cushion for the fluctuation in the prices of the main export products was desirable. It was unanimously agreed that diversification by itself was self-defeating.

One of the most interesting speeches on the economic planning of Malaya that I have ever heard was given by Mr. H.H. King, a Harvard University lecturer, who, at one time, was a lecturer in economics at the Hongkong University. He had been to Malaya and met the Tunku and other leaders of the Alliance. He had written books and given several lectures on the Federation of Malaya. He also was kind enough to present me with a signed copy of his monograph on Malaya. In his speech, Mr. King gave an accurate description of our Five Year Development Plan and his commentary on it was remarkable for its deep insight into the problems now confronting Malaya.

Monday, April 21, 1958

I and my wife went to the reception at the Embassy of the United Arab Republic. The Embassy is typical of most of the embassies of the Arabic countries. It is big, imposing and lavishly furnished. The Ambassador, who gave the party to bid farewell to Washington, since he is returning to Egypt and not returning to Washington, is, I am told, quite popular in Washington.

After the reception, we went to a symphony concert, of which I was one of the patrons. It is the accepted practice in Washington for Ambassadors to be invited to be patrons, for which privilege they are asked to give donations, which make sizeable inroads into their pockets.

After the concert, we went to the reception at the Embassy of Mexico. This Embassy is typical of the embassies of the Latin American countries. It is big, imposing and lavishly furnished. The Treasury officials at home should see these embassies, before they think that ours is expensive.

Tuesday, April 22, 1958

I went to the American University to attend a meeting to acquaint Ambassadors in Washington with the proposed School of International Service at the University, which will be opened in September this year. This school will give two types of courses. One type will grant degrees to students who have attended a full course on foreign service; the other is specially designed for those already in Government service who want to study foreign affairs but who have not the time to attend the full course leading to a degree. It is worth watching how the school develops and it may be advisable to send some of our students or officers to it.

Wednesday, April 23, 1958

In the morning Eric Kocher called in to brief me on his observations of Singapore and the Federation of Malaya, gained during his recent visit to the region.

In Singapore, he was told that Lim Yew Hock would try to get a postponement of the coming election, in order to give his Party more time to prepare and to win support. P.A.P. was almost certain to win the election.[43] The British was prepared to let Yew Hock claim all the credit of past performance. In the event of P.A.P. winning, the British would try their very best to work with it, failing which it would have to bring the military in.

Of the Federation, he said it was like going home again. Kuala Lumpur is a hive of activities and there is general feeling of confidence and peace. In the M.C.A., H.S. Lee is back in power; Ong [Yoke Lin] is out and May [Mrs Ong] has confined herself to her room.[44] H.S. Lee told him that if the

---

[43] The People's Action Party led by Lee Kuan Yew won 43 of 51 seats in the 30 May 1959 elections.
[44] Col. H.S. Lee was made Malaya's first Finance Minister. In 1955 and 1957, he lost control over the MCA's Selangor state branch to Labour and Social Welfare Minister Ong Yoke Lin. Lee successfully backed Lim Chong Eu for party president in the March 1958 party elections. Ong was associated with the defeated faction led by Tan Siew Sin, and consequently lost his position as the party's secretary-general (Tan 1997: 260–61). He became Malaya's permanent representative to the UN 1962–64.

Alliance did not get American aid on the Development Plan, the Alliance would lose the election. Tunku, on the other hand, was not so pessimistic, and said the Alliance would win but with a reduced majority.[45]

He enquired who would present the application for the loan, the American Ambassador in Kuala Lumpur or myself. I said that the Government had not decided yet.

In the afternoon, I gave a talk to trade union leaders of the Electrical and Engineering Industries, who were accompanied by George Weaver, an official of American Federation of Labour. My speech was on the economy of the Federation.

Thursday, April 24, 1958
Friday, April 25 1958

Both days were spent in New York. I gave a dinner for Jacobson of Chase Manhattan Bank, who had visited Malaya. He was sorry to hear of the delay in setting up our Central Bank. Central Bank, according to him, is an attribute of a country's economic independence. He did not see any difficulties at all in setting up a Central Bank. As for the Governor of the Bank, if the Federation Government could pick a senior civil servant interested in economics he could guarantee to get him trained to be Governor of our Central Bank within a matter of weeks. Without a Central Bank, there is no means by which American capital can participate on a large scale in Malayan economy.

After dinner, we went to a Russian ballet. The tumultuous, warm applause which greeted the entire cast after the show was a tribute to American sense of judging foreign culture on its merits, divorced from political prejudice. Managed to deal with the work in New York Office in a matter of hours.

Before leaving for Washington on Saturday, April 26, met Tunku Ja'afar, who had arrived that morning from leave in the Federation. Among other

---

[45] Despite winning only 51.7% of the votes in the 1959 general elections — Malaya's first since independence — the ruling Alliance Party consisting of UMNO, MCA and the Malayan Indian Congress (MIC) managed nevertheless to secure 74 of 104 seats.

things, he informed me that subject to my agreement the Prime Minister had agreed to his transfer to London and that [Mohammad] Sopiee [Sheik Ibrahim] would take his place. I said I had no objection.

Monday, April 28, 1958

Gave a farewell dinner at our Embassy for Ambassador Mehta, who was returning to India on retirement after having served 8 years in Washington. I am very fond of Mehta and so are the other Ambassadors in Washington. He is a good type of Indian, who is charming and makes friends easily. He has done much to put forward India's case in Washington.

Tuesday, April 29, 1958

Attended a reception by the Japanese Ambassador in honour of the Emperor's Birthday. It was a big party. It is the practice of the Embassies in America to celebrate Birthdays of Rulers and National Days. Yet in our case the Treasury has instructed that the item "National Day Celebration" should be deleted from our Budget pending discussion on the subject.

In the evening, went to Kocher's house to attend a dinner in honour of Mr. [Elbridge] Dubrow, American Ambassador to Vietnam. Mr. Dubrow told me that he met our Prime Minister in Vietnam and that the latter was as confident and hearty as usual.

Wednesday, April 30, 1958

Gave an interview to Miss Frances Willard Kerr of U.S.I.A. who is going to write about me and my family for publication in Malaya.[46]

---

[46] The USIA — United States Information Agency — existed from 1953 to 1999. Its functions included increasing understanding and acceptance of US policies and the US society by foreign audiences, broadening dialogue between Americans, American institutions and their counterparts overseas, and increasing US Government knowledge and understanding of foreign attitudes, and their implications for US foreign policy.

Thursday, May 1, 1958

Mr. John D. Rockefeller III called at the Embassy.[47] He had just returned from a trip to the Far East, in the course of which he visited Malaya. He mentioned that when he was in Kuala Lumpur E.C.A.F.E. was in session. He was impressed at the way the Government handled the Conference. He was very grateful to the Prime Minister who, besides including him at a dinner party to which, he said, many distinguished guests were invited, had graciously spared half-an-hour before the dinner to talk to him. He was very impressed by the Prime Minister who, he said, was very clear and firm in his stand. He inquired whether USA had included Malaya in its aid programme. Knowing that he had great influence with the Administration, I ventured to outline to him about our proposal to seek American aid. He himself was quite sure that the Federation of Malaya had a strong case for aid from USA. He said that the USA should give Malaya aid, because Malaya was passing through a transition; the aid given would be a "primer" to Malayan economy, which once it gets moving under present favourable conditions generated by the present Government, would progress rapidly without further help. This is in contrast to the other countries, which had received American aid, where, once aid is given, it must continue to act as a prop to the economy.

During the course of the conversation, the subject of Central Bank was brought up. Mr. Rockefeller was amazed at the delay in setting up our Central Bank, which he was told would take 2 years to establish. He enquired whether we had asked the World Bank to help us.[48]

---

[47] Rockefeller's father, John D. Rockefeller Jr, was the dominant force in Standard Oil (Esso), and was the richest man in the world. He was a major philanthropist, and donated the land along the East River in Manhattan upon which the United Nations headquarters still stands.

[48] According to correspondence written on 28 May 1958 to Ismail, Deputy Prime Minister Abdul Razak Hussein had, upon reading Ismail's argument that a central bank had to be set up as soon as possible, talked to O.A. Spencer, who was the Economic Adviser in the Prime Minister's Department, and Finance Minister H.S. Lee about the matter. Lee then prepared a paper for the Malayan Cabinet, which decided to establish the institution by 1 January 1959 (Letters). In the event, the parliament passed the Central Bank Ordinance of Malaya on 23 October, and Bank Negara, Malaya's central bank, was founded on 26 January 1959 (Ooi 2006: 105).

I mentioned the need of American capital to come to the Federation. He asked whether, if American capital went to Malaya, it would not widen further the gap between the economic position of the Malays and the Chinese. I replied that it was unanimously agreed by all races in Malaya in the long term interest of the prosperity and peace in Malaya that Malays should be given a footing in the economy of the country. I further mentioned that the backwardness of the Malays in the economic section was due to the past policy of the British Administration to absorb all Malays into Government service. On the East Coast of Malaya, Malays have been engaged in business for quite a long time and it is more urgent now than ever before that these Malays should learn the "know-how" of modern business, if they were to successfully compete with the others in the economic life of the country. This is where American capital with its modern outlook, which enables investors, labour, and the country to benefit, can play a useful role in helping the Malays. Further, as he himself had mentioned, British investment in Malaya is not meeting with much competition and as a result has the monopoly in the Federation. For the sake of private enterprise, which really thrives on competition, and for the sake of British investment itself, it is necessary to introduce American capital in order to stimulate competition. Mr. Rockefeller agreed with my contention.

I am deeply impressed with Mr. Rockefeller. He is an unassuming man and his family regards the vast fortune of the Rockefeller as a trust, which must be devoted for the welfare of mankind.

Friday, May 2, 1958

Went to the reception at the Mayflower to celebrate the Birthday of the King of Iraq. It was a grand affair, black tie with lavish food and champagne flowing freely. It must have cost a small fortune. I met an interesting couple, Mr. and Mrs. Fletcher. Mrs. Fletcher is from the South. An attractive woman, she has all the prejudices of a Southerner and still talked of the Yanks waging war on the South. "All we ask", she said, "was the Yanks not to interfere with us."

Monday, May 5, 1958

Arrived in New York accompanied by Ismail [Ali]. The first thing that attracted my attention was that the chromium covers of the wheels of the official car were missing. I was told that Tunku Ja'afar had used the car to take him to the airport on the previous Friday, when he set out on his trip to St. Louis. He had left the car at the airport until he returned late on Sunday. It was during this period that the covers were stolen. I was annoyed that Tunku Ja'afar had such scant respect for Government property.

We went to the United Nations to attend the meeting of the Commission on International Commodities. Our Government has decided that we should stand as a candidate for membership of this organisation at their next meeting, and it was thought it would create a good impression on the members of the Commission and would enhance our chances of being elected if I, as Ambassador to the United Nations, attended as observer at the current session.

Tuesday, May 6, 1958

I and Tunku Ja'afar went to luncheon with Mr. Otto Preminger, a famous film producer, who works independently of the big studios but whose production is in great demand by these giants.[49] He was going to Malaya to investigate whether conditions in Malaya were favourable to his operations there for his new production, especially in regard to the degree of co-operation from the Government officials. I wrote him a letter of introduction to our Prime Minister.

---

[49] Otto Ludwig Preminger directed and produced numerous films from the 1930s to the 1970s, and was twice nominated for an Oscar for Best Director. *Anatomy of a Murder*, both produced and directed by him, was nominated for Best Film in 1959. It is not known whether he ever shot on location in Malaya.

Wednesday, May 7, 1958

Attended a stag dinner at the Mayflower given by the American-Australian Association to honour the Coral Sea Battle.[50] Coral Sea Battle fought during the last war was the turning point in the history of Australia and the war in the Pacific. The Japanese invasion of Australia was defeated. Mr. Beale, the new Australian Ambassador, gave a speech remarkable for its oratory.

Thursday, May 8, 1958

Went with my wife to luncheon at the Australian Embassy. Among those present was Mr. Townley, the Australian Minister of Supply. I had met Mr. Townley in Wellington, when we both attended the Colombo Plan and I took instant liking to him. We talked of elections in our two countries; the Australians are having theirs this year. I jokingly told him that if the Alliance won the next election I would ask the Prime Minister to send me as Ambassador to Australia, to which he seriously replied he very much wished so. It is, perhaps, a reflection that Australia is still smarting under the fact that the Alliance Government had not sent a top man to represent the Federation in Australia. No reflection, of course, on our present High Commissioner, who, I was told at the party, is doing excellent work.

Monday, May 12, 1958

Arrived in New York. With Mr. Ormsby, Chairman of the Rubber Manufacturers Association, went to the office of the United States Rubber Company. Spent about an hour talking to Mr. Cake, Officer-in-Charge of the Research Division, and Mr. Madsen, General Manager, Plantation

---

[50] This battle was fought on May 4–8, 1942 between Japan on one side, and the United States and Australia on the other. For the first time in history, aircraft carriers were arrayed against each other. The Americans lost its carrier, the *Lexington*, while the Japanese lost the *Shōhō*, a light carrier. The Japanese subsequently abandoned their attempt to land troops to take Port Moresby, New Guinea.

Ismail was studying in Melbourne when the battle took place and he would have been quite knowledgeable about this pivotal event.

Division. United States Rubber Company owned about 30,000 acres of rubber in Sumatra and only 3,000 acres in Malaya. The Company is very pessimistic about its future in Indonesia, and is holding on in the hope that events will turn for the better. Both Mr. Cake and Mr. Madsen were very impressed with our rubber replanting programme and with the political climate in the Federation of Malaya. They were very interested to hear that the Government is encouraging the opening up of land for rubber. They were anxious to hear about our views on the Rubber Restriction Scheme. When I told them that we could not commit ourselves to a rubber restriction scheme unless we knew first whether such a scheme would be practicable, in view of the fact that there is now synthetic rubber, they both voiced the opinion that no scheme would be practicable and that it would be against the Federation's interest to support such a scheme in view of her increasing and low-cost production when the replanting scheme matures.

We had lunch with Mr. Humphrey Jr., Board Chairman, and his colleagues. Conversation drifted to the situation in Indonesia, political situation in Singapore and the Federation, and the Prime Minister's suggestion of a charter of freedom for foreign capital in South-East Asia.

After lunch, Mr. Cake took me to see the Company's Research Centre in New Jersey. The capital cost of the centre was US$6 million and the recurrent cost is US$4^1/$_2$ million. Mr. Cake was emphatic that the Company's future was in its research division, and voiced the opinion that if one company could have such a research centre the Federation Government should certainly have one as big. It was really an interesting experience going through the centre, and once again I was impressed by the importance which American enterprise puts on research and [how it] backs it with deeds. A very salutary lesson to business community in Malaya.

Tuesday, May 13, 1958

Spent the morning in New York office. Tunku Ja'afar could not get a release of the lease of the house he is now staying in and which lease was entered in his own name for two years. Poor Tunku Ja'afar, he is incapable of coping with any negotiation without making a mess of it. One of the reasons for his unsatisfactory work in New York is that he lives far away from the office. It took him a good half-hour by train and $1^1/_2$ hours in a car to get to work. Now Sopiee may, as a result of Tunku Ja'afar's mistake, have to occupy the house, which, I must say, is very luxurious, since it is owned by a millionaire, but certainly not suitable for a diplomat, who has to work in New York and with irregular hours of duty.

I had lunch with Mr. Jacobson, Mr. Kelly, both of whom are working with Chase Manhattan Bank, and Mr. McKittrick, who had been specially invited by Mr. Jacobson on my request. Mr. McKittrick is a retired banker who specialised in Central Banks. He was sent by the World Bank to investigate into India's Five-Year Plan. He knows the London market very well and is well versed in London banks and the Bank of England. He had read Keynes-Watson Report on the Central Bank in Malaya. On the whole he agreed with the Report, except on the question of separate currencies if two central banks were established and on the question of holding all our currency backing in sterling. On the former, he said, if a separate currency was established, the Federation of Malaya currency would still be known to the world as Malayan currency, and only currencies of Singapore and Borneo territories would have new names unfamiliar to the world; on the second, he thought that our currency backing should be distributed according to the ratio of the destination of our export products. For example, if our trade in rubber and tin is distributed two-thirds in the Sterling Area and one-third in the Dollar Area, then our currency backing should be held in the two areas in accordance with this ratio. I was struck by Mr. McKittrick's simplicity, and what a wonderful man to get as first Governor of our Central Bank.

Thursday, May 15, 1958

Bugbee of the Natural Rubber Bureau called at the Chancery to tell me of an advertisement for the post of Controller of Rubber, a very important post for the Rubber Industry. If such autonomous organisations as Natural Rubber Bureau and Tin Bureau could be sent important notices as the one mentioned above, why could not our Embassy in USA be also sent copies? Ultimately, inquiries are inevitably made at our Embassy, and it is embarrassing for the Embassy to admit that it has no knowledge on the subject at all.

From the discussion with Bugbee, it is clear that, because of remuneration offered, no candidates from USA will be forthcoming. In USA, men of the calibre mentioned in the advertisement are extremely well paid by the Rubber Manufacturers. For example, Mr. Cake of the United States Rubber Company, in charge of the research section, is paid $75,000 annually. It is, therefore, an open field for candidates from the United Kingdom. The important consideration is whether a suitable man will get the job. From my discussion with Bugbee, the important consideration in selecting the candidates is that the prospective candidate in addition to his other qualifications, must have a training which can make him appreciate and know the works of research.

Friday, May 16, 1958

The Minister, Ismail, left for Malaya for briefing as leader of our delegation to the conference of officials in London to prepare the Papers for the Commonwealth Economic Ministerial Conference to be held in Ottawa later in the year. During the 8 months that Ismail has been here, he has been away twice from Washington to lead delegations from Malaya. Because of this and the fact that Malaya is not ready with the preparation of attracting American capital, I recommend that Ismail, who is a senior official and a very capable one, should return to Malaya to assume a post worthy of his ability.

In the evening, I received the documents from External Affairs to be submitted to the Secretary of State. I contacted Kocher straightaway, and thus initiated the difficult process of securing an appointment with the Secretary.

Sunday, May 18, 1958

Together with Eric Kocher and his wife, I and my wife made a two-hour journey to Richmond to attend a luncheon party given by Walter Robertson, Assistant Secretary of State for Far Eastern Affairs. This function is an annual affair to which all Ambassadors of the Far East countries and their wives are invited.

The Robertson's house is a beautiful structure built on the line of the old type of houses, so characteristic of the South, with their wide frontage, and numerous small rooms which are quaint and picturesque but at the same time a nightmare to the housewives. The house is situated on a hill on the bank of the River James and commands a wonderful view. The guests roamed over the luscious green lawn in front of the house and were well served with Mint Julep, a drink characteristic of the South. It was at this time that Carlos Romulo, Ambassador of Philippines, gave Mr. Robertson a surprise by decorating him, on behalf of the Philippines Government, with a high order of the Philippines.[51]

Luncheon was served on small tables, which are casually distributed throughout all the rooms. This arrangement is characteristic of receptions given by Americans in Washington and is copied by many Ambassadors, It has the advantage of overcoming problems on protocol.

Altogether, we had a pleasant day in the South.

Wednesday, May 21, 1958

With my wife, arrived in Dallas, in the State of Texas, at noon after $4^1/_2$ hours flight from Washington. In the same plane were the Ambassador of Brazil, his wife and his two Secretaries and their wives. We had been invited by the Dallas Council of World Affairs as their guests for the World Affairs Week in Dallas. The next day, the Ambassador of Japan and his Secretary and other dignitaries joined the party.

Dallas airport, which was opened only a few weeks before our arrival, is the finest I have seen, and I was told that it was the finest in America. It is all air-conditioned, and has beautiful dining rooms, lounges, and shops which display "cowboy" goods.

We were interviewed by pressmen and T.V. men, and were taken to our hotel — the Baker Hotel, where more newspapermen interviewed me. Without exception, they showed an utter lack of knowledge of the Federation

---

[51] Carlos Romulo was president of the UN General Assembly in 1949–50 and was an unsuccessful candidate for the post of UN Secretary-General in 1953, losing to Dag Hammarskjöld.

of Malaya, and mistook the Federation for Indonesia and kept on asking me of the civil war in Indonesia.

In the evening, we were entertained by a Dallas family Mr. and Mrs. Schrimp. Mr. Schrimp is an architect. In the party were a lawyer, whom everyone insisted on calling "judge" and his wife, and two other couples — one, an insurance man and his wife; the other, an oilman and his wife. We had barbecue in the backyard under a porch. Mr. Schrimp is an expert at barbecue, because it certainly was the best broiled steak I have ever tasted in America. During the course of the conversation, Mr. Schrimp, who, I imagine, represents quite a section of opinion in Texas, was very anti American aid programme. He said that Americans had to bear heavy taxation as a result of this programme, and if not for the heavy taxation in America he and others like him would be well off. He had to work very hard to earn what he did and many Americans developed heart disease and died young because they had to work hard to feed their families. It sickened him and others like him when they read about American aid abused by the recipients and never reached the peoples of the country for whom the aid was intended. The "judge", who had travelled widely and been to Malaya, and who is going to Europe and Russia soon, was even more emphatic, and said that the quickest way to solve the present world problems was to go to war with Russia and that he was confident USA would lick the Russians. He had served in the Guadal-Canal, and man for man he was convinced that an American was the superior to anyone else. When I told him that the next war would mean the end of the world, he just laughed.

Thursday, May 22, 1958

At luncheon, I addressed the Salesmanship Club and the Dallas Council of World Affairs. My subject was "Malaya's Role in International Affairs and World Trade".

In the evening, I went to the International Dinner. The guest speaker was Mr. Christian Herter, Under Secretary of State. He spoke in defence of American aid programme. In the course of his speech, he mentioned that USA emerged as the leader of the free world not of its own choice but rather it was thrust upon her. He said that USA embarked on its foreign aid programme not to seek praise but rather to do her duty to the free world. Inevitably, for such a huge programme there was bound to be abuse, but on the whole it was administered effectively. Further, he added, American aid programme was not given according to USA like and dislike of certain Governments. It was given according to the merits of a case. Otherwise USA would be accused of interfering in the internal affairs of other nations. I have always had an admiration for Herter, but this was the first time that I had heard him speak. It is good that USA has leaders like him. I was told that he was loved and revered by Americans.[52]

Friday, May 23, 1958

We were invited to the Wichita Falls, a town, two hours drive in a car. In the evening we were entertained to Chuck Wagon dinner. This is a dinner held according to the custom of old pioneer days. Food is cooked beside a wagon, which is specially used for carrying food for the caravan. The hospitality was spontaneous, and this is true wherever one goes in Texas. There were folk dances, mock gun duels, etc..

Saturday, May 24, 1958

We made a tour of ranches and oil fields. During this tour, we got an excellent idea of the riches of Texas, and hence the fabulously rich Texan oil men and cattle ranchers. Practically, all the ranches that we saw have oil wells, and the slow rhythmic motion of oil pumps was a familiar sight. One ranch was fabulously rich. It had air-conditioned barns for the cattle, and we were shown one pedigree bull, which was about to be sold for US$20,000. The owner had sold 6 recently for US$250,000. One rancher had 83,000 acres of ranch land plus oil fields, and he was worth US$200 million! Yes, Texas is as rich as Croesus.

---

[52] Herter was Governor of Massachusetts in 1953–56, and succeeded John Foster Dulles as American Secretary-of-State in 1959.

Monday, May 26, 1958

At 12 o'clock, accompanied by Mr. Lim [Taik Choon], First Secretary of our Embassy, went to the State Department for an interview with Mr. Dulles, Secretary of State.[53] We were met at the entrance by Mr. Swezey, officer in charge of Malayan desk at the State Department. We were escorted to the Secretary of State's Office, where we saw several reporters loitering about. We were told that they were there to glean news of events, which were in the limelight at the moment — news of events in France and in North Africa. They showed signs of curiosity at our appearance. Mr. Lim stayed to parry with them, and I later found out that he did very well, telling them nothing.

Our appointment was for 12.30 p.m., but the Secretary of State did not see us until 12.40 p.m.. It was very difficult to get an appointment with him, because, firstly, he was always busy and, secondly, the procedure as instructed to me was unprecedented. The business, in which I was to see the Secretary of State, was within the competence of the Assistant Secretary of State, Mr. Walter Robertson. The name "Assistant Secretaries", as applied to the officials of the State Department, is a misnomer, because, unlike Assistant Secretaries in other countries, those in the State Department of U.S.A. have wide powers, including the power to appear before a Committee of Congress.

While waiting for our appointment, we were joined by Walter Robertson. It was he, who was really instrumental in securing the appointment for me.

The Secretary of State saw me with Mr. Robertson and Mr. Swezey. This was the second time that I saw the Secretary of State; the first time was about 8 months ago when I presented my credentials. For a man of 70, and one

---

[53] The Tunku had, in a letter dated 2 May, asked Dr Ismail to call on the Secretary of State to "present to him our case orally and to deposit with him before you leave, an *aide memoire* which is being forwarded to you" (see Appendix 3). The Tunku was afraid that if he contacted Dulles directly, and the request for aid was denied, both parties would be placed in an awkward position (Letters).

Dr Ismail did as the Tunku had suggested, but later informed the Prime Minister that the procedure was "unprecedented". Normally, the aid-seeking party first meets the Assistant Secretary responsible for the region in which the former's country is situated, who then presents the case before the American Congress. Dr Ismail admitted to the Tunku at this time that he was getting "tired and weary with rushing about", and wished for a 3–4 weeks' holiday once the loan negotiation was done (Letters 26 May 1958).

who has been operated on for cancer of the intestines, he looked remarkably well and strong.[54]

I gave an oral presentation of our application for loans, taking about 10 minutes to do so. The Secretary of State was flabbergasted to hear the amount of M$455 million, and remarked that USA resources were not unlimited. When told that we expected to have deficits in the Budgets of 1958 and 1959 amounting to M$150 and M$160 million respectively, he asked whether I knew what the deficits in his Government's Budgets were. I said yes, but added that without the cost of the Emergency amounting to M$126 million annually and with the establishment of a Central Bank which would facilitate the expansion of floating debt operation and assist our Government in its long term debt operation, we would also be able to get along with Budgetary deficits as the USA [did]. He expressed his appreciation of our Government's firm stand against Communism and without giving any commitment, his Government would sympathetically consider our application. He asked that the documents of our application should be left with Mr. Dillon, who would be asked to make an appointment with me. (See Appendix 3)

I am to see Dillon, who is Under Secretary of State, any time after June 4.

Tuesday, May 27, 1958

Arrived in Minneapolis at about noon and proceeded to Hotel Leamington, where I was booked in and also where many of the offices of W.H.O. during the Session were situated.

I was told by the Information Centre of W.H.O. that Dr. Mohd Din, Deputy Director of Medical Services, Federation of Malaya, the other delegate to the W.H.O. Conference and who was asked to take with him my credentials, had not arrived. I asked Dr. Coigne, a high official of W.H.O., whether I

---

[54] John Foster Dulles died of cancer in May 1959. He was a major "Cold War warrior" who helped to build up the North Atlantic Treaty Organization (NATO), and was a force behind the 1951 military alliance between Australia, New Zealand and the United States (ANZUS). He was also the architect of SEATO, the defence pact signed in 1954 between the United States, Australia, Britain, France, New Zealand, Pakistan, the Philippines and Thailand.

could attend the afternoon Session without having submitted my credentials. He said I could. The failure to transmit the credentials of our delegates well before the Session was embarrassing and created a bad impression for our country, which had just been admitted a member. I could not understand why my credentials, at least, could not have been sent earlier and independently of Dr. Din.

The afternoon meeting was the last meeting of the Commemorative Session of W.H.O., which was celebrating its tenth anniversary. It started the day before and our seats were vacant and very noticeable, since we were a new member. I could not be present on the first day, because I had to see the Secretary of State in order to submit our application for American loans. Dr. Din, having cut very fine the time-table of his arrival, was delayed and did not arrive until the night of my arrival.

Wednesday, May 28, 1958
Thursday, May 29, 1958

I met Dr. Din and was appalled to hear that he had brought no briefs with him. At the morning Session, I was told to say something about our membership. I had perforce to get up and say something.

The plenary Session of W.H.O. continued the debate on the Report of the Director-General. I told Dr. Din that I had to go back to Washington, but advised him that he should make an attempt to speak at the forthcoming meetings of the Session, because, firstly, as a new member we must make ourselves heard and, secondly, since our contribution is much bigger than other countries, we must at least make our needs clear to other member countries.

Friday, May 30, 1958

Returned to Washington.

Monday, June 2, 1958

Arrived in New York. Discussed with Sopiee the problems of his taking over from Tunku Ja'afar. Sopiee mentioned that there are quite a number of decisions which were taken by Tunku Ja'afar without formal approval from me as Permanent Representative. I was not at all surprised, because since he had been in New York Office, Tunku Ja'afar had always acted as if he were the Permanent Representative. I told Sopiee that if he would put all the actions which had been taken by Tunku Ja'afar, in proper minutes form, I would do all that is possible to regularise matters.

In the evening, I gave Tunku Ja'afar and his wife a farewell party, to which Sopiee and his wife were also invited.

Tuesday, June 3, 1958

I went to luncheon given by the Chairman of the Board of Pacific Tin, a mining company operating in Malaya, the manager of which is Norman Cleaveland, whom I know very well. There were many people connected with mining present, and one of them, a Mr. Smith, is the editor of the powerful magazine, the *American Metal*.

Mr. Thiele, the Chairman of the Board, in the course of the luncheon mentioned that his company, being American and therefore a competitor to the other mining companies in Malaya, mainly British, was discriminated against in the allocation of quotas under the Domestic Tin Restriction Scheme. I asked him whether Norman Cleaveland was a member of the Central Committee, which allocates quotas. He said no, and that the members were mainly British, especially the Anglo-Oriental group. I told him that if he had grounds for being discriminated against, he should petition the Minister of Natural Resources,[55] who, I am sure, will redress the grievances.

In the evening, I and my wife acted as host and hostess at our function at New York to celebrate the Birthday of the Paramount Ruler.[56] It was a most disappointing affair. With the exception of Sopiee, Lim the Second Secretary, and Kumar the Document Officer, all the other members of the staff arrived late. Tunku Ja'afar and his wife excused themselves by saying that they were busy packing as they were leaving the next day. There was no

---

[55] Bahaman bin Shamsuddin.
[56] This was Tuanku Abdul Rahman ibni Almarhum Tuanku Muhammad, the Sultan of Negri Sembilan. Tunku Ja'afar is his second son.

announcer, so that I and my wife had either to pretend to know or to ask the guests their names. It was most embarrassing. The whole party was arranged by one person — Miss Watson, the Stenographer. It is just as well that Tunku Ja'afar is now in London, and I only pray God that Tunku Ya'acob will get on better with him.[57]

Wednesday, June 4, 1958

Back at Washington. In the evening, I and my wife were host and hostess at our Embassy for the celebration of the Paramount Ruler's Birthday. In contrast to New York, this was a superb party. It was well organised and the guests were very pleased indeed with the reception. The staff in Washington had worked as a team to make the function a success.

Wednesday, June 11, 1958

Went to see Mr. Dillon, Deputy Under-Secretary for Economic Affairs. He was supported by his colleagues, among whom I recognised Eric Kocher, Swezey of Malayan Desk, and Mr. Palmer. Mr. Dillon asked me if I had anything to add to what I had told Secretary of State Dulles. I said that I would like to stress that help, if given, would be once and for all. Further, if the Government had to cut back on its Development Plan, it would be very unfortunate in view of the fact that General Elections would be held sometime in the middle of next year. I have no doubt that the Alliance Government would win the Elections, but it may not be able to have an effective majority in Parliament. If such be the case, then a coalition Government would be set up and demand for coming to a truce with the Communists in the Jungle

---

[57] Around this time, Dr Ismail received a letter from Deputy Premier Abdul Razak Hussein. After discussing the setting up of the Central Bank, Razak told Dr Ismail that they could not as yet find a good replacement for Ismail Ali in Washington. Dr Ismail had earlier told Razak that he thought Ismail Ali's talents were being wasted at his posting. Razak had in turn been told that Dr Ismail was overworked and in need of rest, and hastened to assure the latter that his suspicions that the Tunku wanted him to stay on longer in Washington and New York were unfounded (Letters).

with the concomitant recognition of Communist Party and demand for the acceptance of help from U.S.S.R. would be irresistible.[58]

Mr. Dillon said that the financial crisis in Malaya is unique, in that it is a cash crisis and not a balance of payment or foreign exchange crisis. As such, help from I.M.F. and Import and Export Bank is precluded. However, he thinks that it is possible to meet our request, though not to the full extent asked for, by making use of the "tools" available to the Administration, by analysing our Development Plan. He stressed that, because of the policy laid down by Congress, Government to Government loans [are] out of the question.

After taking my leave of Mr. Dillon, I went with Eric Kocher, Swezey and Lim, our First Secretary, to Eric Kocher's office. There we discussed the procedure to be followed. When Eric told me that the American Embassy in Kuala Lumpur would probably have enough economic staff, I suggested that the initial dissection of the Development Plan should be done in Kuala Lumpur, to be followed later, if necessary, in Washington. He was going to explore this suggestion.

I sent a cable home containing a report of the interview as described above, adding a further suggestion of my own that talks between our representatives and the American representatives should also embrace specific projects on police and military, as was done, I was told, with Burma. I received a cable back asking for a description of what was done with Burma. I am seeking an interview with the Burmese Ambassador.[59]

---

[58] The Americans were aware that popular support for the Alliance government in Malaya was weakening at a crucial time. An American policy paper from 28 May 1958 stated that "this deterioration in the government's political strength, particularly among Chinese and Indian voters supporting neutralist-oriented parties favouring recognition of Communist China and the Malayan Communist Party, could neutralize the progress made in achieving US objectives in Malaya" (Sodhy 1991: 189).

[59] Dr Ismail had met the Burmese Ambassador by 17 June. What he learned, and what he told Defence Minister Razak, was how vitally important it was to concentrate on "Specific Projects of Security" when applying for American loans. For example, the Burmese had been successful in getting American aid for a "police project", so what Malaya could do, according to Dr Ismail, was to perhaps concentrate on an "Air Force" project that would include specifics on training schemes, equipment, airfields and the like (Letters).

Friday, June 13, 1958

Sir Harold Caccia dropped in at our Embassy in response to my request to see him at the British Embassy the following day, which unfortunately could not be arranged. I told him of our approach to U.S.A. for loans, reiterating our Government's gratefulness of help which U.K. has given and is giving. I promised to let him have copies of documents on the loans as soon as we received further copies from home.[60]

Monday, June 16, 1958

Copies of documents on loans arrived. A set was dispatched to the British Ambassador.

Thursday, June 19, 1958

I arrived in New York in my own car with my family, on our way for a fortnight holidays in Cape Cod.

I spent the afternoon working in our New York Office. Sopiee is turning up work for me more regularly than Tunku Ja'afar, and he has introduced order and discipline in the office.

In the evening we went to dinner, after which the theatre with the Delsons. Mr. [Robert] Delson is a lawyer to several Far Eastern embassies, such as Indonesia and Burma. He told us that he had just returned from Jakarta. His information was that there would be a reshuffle of the Cabinet and that Moekarto, the Indonesian Ambassador to Washington, who was

---

Dr Ismail's efforts did pay off. Three months after his return to Malaya, his successor, Nik Kamil, signed an agreement — on 18 March 1959 — with the American government for two Development Loan Fund grants worth US$20 million, for the North Klang Straits deepwater port project and the construction of roads and bridges. Support for the teaching hospital scheme was disallowed.

[60] Incidentally, Caccia is credited with the famous quotation purportedly made while he was the British ambassador in Washington: "If you are to stand up for your government you must be able to stand up to your government" (*Columbia World of Quotations* 1996).

then on leave in Indonesia, would be the likely choice as Foreign Minister. Delson had heard of our approach for a loan from the USA, and he offered his services, if required. He had performed similar services to Indonesia and Burma.

Friday, June 20, 1958

I gave a talk to a group of businessmen on our policy to attract foreign capital. It was well received. Sopiee cabled the text of the speech home.

Saturday, June 21, 1958

Left New York for Cape Cod.

Monday, July 7, 1958

Returned from holidays.

Tuesday, July 8, 1958

Started work in Embassy.

Thursday, July 10, 1958

Went with my wife to New York.

Went with Sopiee to a meeting of Afro-Asian at United Nations, at which I signed on behalf of the Federation Government a sponsorship of the application of the Afro-Asian countries to include the question of Algeria on the Agenda of the 13th Assembly of United Nations. At the end of the meeting, Lall of India approached me and asked whether we would consider being a co-sponsorship of an application to include the question of racial conflict in South Africa on the Agenda of the 13th Assembly of United Nations. I told him that as soon as I had studied the draft application, I would give him my answer. Back at our New York Office, I studied with Sopiee the text of the application, and after making it clear to Lall that our sponsorship, if approved by the Federation Government, would not imply that we would be committed to future steps on the subject, I instructed Sopiee to cable home, recommending our sponsorship of the application.

Sopiee mentioned that he had been sounding various delegations on the chances of our being elected to one of the Vice Presidencies of the United Nations and asked what I thought of the idea. I told him I would think of the subject.

In the evening I and my wife went to dinner with Sir Claude Corea [Ceylon's new Permanent Secretary to the UN] and Lady Corea and, in fact, this was the reason why my wife accompanied me on this trip. Sir Claude Corea and Lady Corea lived in a well furnished apartment, the rent of which, I was told, was no more than what we paid for the house in which Tunku Ja'afar lived and now occupied by Sopiee. Besides being well furnished, it is well situated within handy distance from United Nations for entertainment.

Sir Claude knows our Prime Minister, having met him in London through a mutual friend. He has a great respect for our Prime Minister; and liked him especially for his spontaneity and natural grace. Sir Claude is a different man from Sir Gunewardene, the former Permanent Representative of Ceylon, in that the former is less talkative and more refined. We had an altogether lovely time.

Friday, July 11, 1958

Among the guests at Sir Claude's party was a Reuters representative, Mr. Christmas Hudson. He informed me that the Afro-Asian was going to discuss Malaya the next week. This naturally intrigued me, and so the next day I asked Sopiee about it. His assumption was that it probably would consider our proposal to stand as one of the Vice Presidencies. I told Sopiee that I had decided not to stand, and my reasons were as follows. We are a new nation, and it is presumptuous to aspire for such a prestige-bearing post as the Vice-Presidency. Our association with the Afro-Asian, until recently, was marked with hesitancy, and this had not escaped the attention of the Group. Therefore, all in all, it would be better to await at least another year.

In the afternoon we took the plane for Washington. Normally the flight took only one hour, but, because of the storm the plane had to divert its course and we were flying for four hours before we landed in Washington. Such occurrences are by no means new, especially in Winter, when I had to make frequent flights to and from Washington/New York. We had asked sometime ago that we should be insured, but up to now no word of reply.

Monday, July 14, 1958 — Monday, July 21, 1958

The dominant feature of this period was undoubtedly the events in the Middle East. The centre of the stage was the meeting room of the Security Council in the United Nations. The gallery, which normally is never filled to capacity, was full.

Lobbyists from the Permanent Missions were as busy as bees and, as was to be expected, the busiest lobbyist was Lall of India. Sopiee, our First Secretary, was in his element, and what he lacked in experience he made up for it in enthusiasm. The best time to judge a person is when he is confronted with an emergency situation, for then his suppressed qualities come up to the surface. Ever since he arrived he has at great pains tried to create an impression that he is a loyal civil servant, prepared to submerge his own feelings and views, in order to carry out impartially the official policy and instructions from the Chief of Mission. I must admit that, except for one occasion, he has so far succeeded. However, the lobby of the United Nations is full of temptation, and Sopiee succumbed. I only noticed it when he surreptitiously disobeyed my instruction. He had received a telegram from External, which contained a press release of our Government's stand, as decided by Cabinet, on the situation in the Middle East. In addition, there was also in the telegram a paragraph, not part of the press release but for the information of our Missions abroad, to the effect that the Prime Minister had called the United Kingdom High Commissioner and the American Ambassador in the Federation to express his deep concern at the landing of American and British troops in Lebanon and Jordan respectively. This information, when released as part of the press statement, gave an entirely different meaning to the press release. Sopiee, I think, favoured this different meaning, as it accorded with his own views, and that was the reason why in circulating our Government press release he included the extra paragraph. When I asked him, he gave the excuse that his interpretation was that the whole content of the telegram was a press release. Coming from a person of lesser intelligence than him, I would have accepted the excuse.[61]

In the Security Council, the United States tried to justify its armed intervention on the grounds that American armed forces had entered Lebanon at the request of the Lebanese Government and in order to protect American lives. The Government of the United Kingdom gave almost the same reasons, but omitted that of trying to protect British lives in Jordan, for its armed intervention in Jordan. The Soviet Union assailed the actions of these two Powers, and charged them with acts of aggression and intervention in internal affairs of Lebanon and Jordan. U.A.R. denied that she was intervening in the affairs of Lebanon and Jordan. Lebanon and Jordan confirmed that the entry of American and British troops into their respective countries was at their invitation to help them resist aggression from U.A.R..

It is my belief that America had gone into Lebanon because she was sure that the success of the revolution in Iraq would be followed by revolutions in Jordan and in Lebanon, and without the presence of her troops in Lebanon these revolutions would have succeeded. She was convinced that these revolutions were designed, encouraged and supported by U.A.R..[62] The British, of course, supported the American action, because she knew that if Jordan and Lebanon went the same way as Iraq she might as well say good-bye to the Middle-East oil.[63]

---

[61] Sopiee was a founding member of the Malayan Labour Party, with views that were more leftist than those publicly held by the Tunku's regime (Ooi 2006: 116).

[62] American President Eisenhower responded to the so-called Lebanon Crisis through Operation Blue Bat, in which 14,000 soldiers were sent in to secure Beirut on 15 July 1958. Lebanon's Christian President Camille Chamoun, fearing a Muslim rebellion seeking for Lebanon to join the UAR, and shocked by the fall of the pro-Western regime in Iraq, had requested American aid. The Americans withdrew on 25 October the same year after having persuaded President Chamoun to resign and allow the moderate Christian general Fuad Chehab to replace him. In what was considered a highly successful operation; the Americans lost one soldier to a sniper, and three were killed in accidents.

[63] The British-supported Hashemite monarchy in Iraq was toppled in a military coup d'etat known as the 14th July Revolution. The uprising was led by Brigadier-General Abd al-Karim Qasim, who became Prime Minister and Defense Minister. Iraq subsequently withdrew from the 3-year-old pro-Western Baghdad Pact and established friendly ties with the Soviet Union. The pact, whose other signatories were Turkey, Iran, Pakistan and the United Kingdom, came to be known as CENTO — Central Treaty Organisation.

Without doubt, events in the Middle East are manifestations of Arab nationalism, which is personified in Nasser. It has taken a violent form, because peaceful, democratic means of expression was denied to it by the support which Western Powers had given to feudalism in the region. It is indeed a sad fact that Americans, who believe in nationalism, had to fight it in defence of Imperialism and Feudalism.

The question now is how far can nationalism, once it has assumed a destructive form, go? Can it be induced to assume a constructive form? As to the first question, I am definite it will spread far and wide, bringing misery and destruction in its path, before finally dying out. As to the second question, I am sure it can, provided America uses her strength and influence against Imperialism and Feudalism, or at the very least refusing to support them and supporting nationalism instead. However, unfortunately solutions to international problems have to take into account such questions as Alliances and sensitivity of members of the Alliances. The American foreign policy is based on the containment of the Communists, and it was in pursuance of this policy that regional pacts such as N.A.T.O. and S.E.A.T.O. were formed and the Eisenhower Doctrine was formulated.[64] The premise, on which this policy was based, was that if Communist aggression was halted, two things would happen. Firstly, negotiations on international problems, such as Disarmament and the Middle East questions, could be entered into with the Russians, who would only negotiate if they know that they have been thwarted in their aims by armed resistance. Secondly, ultimately the Russian people would get tired of futile Russian expansionist policy and would start a movement of liberalising the regime and thereby changing Russian policy [to one] more suited to peaceful co-existence. The motive of American policy of containment is self-preservation. Americans have no imperialistic designs,

---

[64] The Truman Doctrine proclaimed on 12 March 1947 is sometimes used to mark the start of the Cold War. The North Atlantic Treaty Organization (NATO) was formed on 4 April 1949 and the Southeast Asian Treaty Organisation (SEATO) on 8 September 1954. The Eisenhower Doctrine was declared to the United States Congress when Eisenhower started his second term in office in January 1957. As a principle of foreign policy, it proclaimed that aid in various forms would be given to countries openly and actively opposed to communism. More specifically, it was a response to the power vacuum created by the decline of British and French power in the oil-rich Middle East, and to the rising influence exerted by Gamel Abdel Nasser and the UAR.

and of this I am convinced. However, implementation of this policy as manifested in regional pacts, which I have mentioned above, attract strange bed-fellows. The British, the Dutch, the French and the Belgians are all colonial powers and they expect the Americans to support them, or at the very least to remain neutral when colonial problems crop up. Therefore, resentment against Americans [is] based on this fact. Many Afro-Asian countries, such as Indonesia, the Arab countries are antagonistic towards Americans, because Americans either remain neutral or move in support of colonial powers or forces which are allied to colonial powers, such as the decadent Arab monarchs and corrupt governments.

The Federation Government policy of neutralism and her belief in the United Nations as an organ for the settlement of international dispute must take account of the intricacies of [the] international situation. To implement the policy of neutralism is not easy. It requires constant vigilance and fine judgment. Otherwise she would be accused of neutralism partial to certain countries. India has already been dubbed "neutral as far as Russia is concerned".

The Security Council has adjourned discussion on the problems of Middle East pending the result of the Summit Meeting in the Security Council of Heads of States.

The Federation Government has issued the following instructions to its Permanent Mission to the United Nations:

(1) The Permanent Representative is to support any motion or, in its absence to initiate one, for the convening of the Emergency Meeting of the Assembly.
(2) At the Emergency Meeting of the Assembly, if necessary, to move a motion referring the problems of the Middle East to the Security Council urging the Council to take cognizance of the urgency of the problems and to come to satisfactory solutions.
(3) If the Security Council failed, then and only then, the Assembly should accept a motion, which would ask member countries to assume individual responsibilities.

In practice, the Permanent Representative can only initiate the convening of the Assembly by invoking "Uniting for Peace Resolution". This resolution was passed by the Security Council, when it met to discuss the Korean question in 1951. At that time the Security Council was powerless to help Korea, because of repeated vetoes by the Soviet Union. It was only when the Soviet Union made the mistake of boycotting the Council that a resolution, called "Uniting for Peace Resolution" was passed by General Assembly. Before this resolution was passed, by virtue of the Charter, the General Assembly could not meet to discuss a problem affecting peace and security, if the problem was seized by the Security Council. The effect of the resolution was that the Assembly could meet to discuss a problem affecting peace and security even though the problem was seized by the Security Council. It also implied that the assembly would meet to pass a resolution which required two-thirds majority to take *effective steps* towards solving the problem. In other words, it could not meet just for the purpose of passing a resolution to refer back the problem to the Security Council, urging the latter to take cognizance of the seriousness of the problem. And yet this is precisely what the Federation Government wanted its Permanent Representative to do. To illustrate how impossible it is to carry out this instruction, it is necessary to trace the necessary steps to be taken. First of all the Permanent Representative must lobby to get at least 41 members to append their signatures in the petition to convene the Assembly under "Uniting for Peace Resolution". In order to get this, he must explain the object of calling the meeting and the nature of the resolution, which he proposes to introduce in the Assembly. He will, of course, have to say that in the first instance, he would move a resolution to refer back the problem to the Security Council, asking the latter to take cognizance of the seriousness of the situation and to find a satisfactory solution. In the event of the Security Council failing to find solutions, the Assembly, which in the meanwhile is kept going simultaneously as the Council is meeting to deliberate on the problem, will be asked to pass a resolution to take effective steps to solve the problem, which would require member countries to shoulder responsibilities.

The result of the efforts of the Permanent Representative to carry out the instruction of the Federation Government would be to bring ridicule to the Government. No member can believe that the Representative of the Federation of Malaya is seriously proposing to convene the Assembly, just for the primary purpose of referring the Middle East problem to the Security Council, urging the latter to take cognizance of the seriousness of the situation. They have seen the Permanent Representative of Malaya sitting with them as observer in the Security Council, sometimes well into the night, and surely the Permanent Representative of Malaya must have been impressed, as they have been, as to the urgency and seriousness with which the Security Council treated the Middle East problem.

Tuesday, July 22, 1958

Went to meet Ong Yoke Lin at the New York International Airport and flew with him to Washington.[65] In the evening I gave a cocktail at the Embassy which was attended by over 100 guests.

Wednesday, July 23, 1958

Went to New York to give a talk on the Federation of Malaya at our New York Office to a group of students of international affairs.

Friday, July 25, 1958

Attended dinner given by the Prime Minister of Ghana. Read a joint communiqué issued in connection with the visit of the Prime Minister of Ghana, in which, among other things, it was stated that USA would consider helping Ghana to improve her economy.[66]

---

[65] Ong became Malaysia's Permanent Representative to the UN and Ambassador to the USA in 1962. He was elected President of the Malaysia Senate in 1973.

[66] Prime Minister Kwame Nkrumah is considered the founder of Ghana, which gained independence on 6 March 1957, six months before Malaya. Nkrumah was toppled by a military coup in February 1966 while he was visiting Vietnam. Ismail was convinced in the early 1950s that Malaya had to gain independence the same way Ghana was doing it, i.e. by holding national elections that are eventually won by the party fighting for independence (Drifting c7).

I have studied the events which led to the visit of the Prime Minister to USA, studied the communiqué on the visit, and come to the conclusion that the events occurred as planned by Ghana.

Sometime ago, the Finance Minister of Ghana visited USA. On a motor-car trip from New York to Washington, and accompanied by his Ambassador, he stopped at a restaurant in a district, which was well-known for its segregation. He was refused a drink and the incident became headline news. In order to make amends, the President of USA invited him to breakfast, and pictures of him and the President at the White House appeared in newspapers. Not long after, the Prime Minister was invited to be a State Guest of the American Government. He came alone. After talking with President Eisenhower, his Finance Minister and Economic Adviser were sent for, and they came accompanied by the Minister of Information. As a result, economic help was offered, giving the impression that help was offered rather [than] sought after.

Monday, July 28, 1958 — Saturday, August 2, 1958

Went to Vancouver to attend a Seminar on Malaya, sponsored by the Extension Branch of the University of British Columbia. The Minister, Inche Ismail, accompanied me. There was doubt, at one stage, whether I would be able to make the trip, because of events in the Middle East, which would make it necessary to convene a Special Session of UN Assembly. However, I was glad that I was able to go, as the following account of the Seminar will reveal.

The University of British Columbia is situated in one of the finest sites I have ever seen. It is on a hill, overlooking the Fraser River, beyond which the blueness of the mountain blends harmoniously with the blue-whiteness of the sky. The buildings are beautifully spaced out, so that the campus, especially that part of it in front of the University, is rich with green lawns.

The Seminar was held in the library on one of the top floors, and to reach it one has to climb a flight of 72 steps. The Chairman of the Seminar was Mr. Selman, Assistant Director of the Extension Division of the University. The staff of the Seminar consisted of myself, Inche Ismail, Mr. Carson the Canadian Trade Commissioner to Malaya, Miss Turnbull a lecturer in history at the University of Malaya, and Dr. McCombie the Director of Dental Services of British Columbia, who had been to Malaya under the Colombo Plan. I spoke on the "Constitution of Malaya" and "Foreign Policy"; Ismail spoke on "Foreign Trade"; Mr. Carson on "Federation and Singapore Trade with Canada"; Dr. McCombie on "Public Health in the Federation"; Miss Turnbull spoke on "History of Malaya", the period covering her early history up to Independence, "Politics in Malaya" and "Singapore — Past and Present".

The speakers, except Miss Turnbull, gave a fairly good account of Malaya in their talks. Miss Turnbull, unfortunately, consented to talk on subjects on which she knew only the British point of view. She was so biased and prejudiced in her lectures that she was only restrained by the presence of myself and Ismail. Her lectures were based entirely on accounts written in English, the sources of which are either the official files of the former Chief Secretary's Office or the English newspapers. In some instances, her information was rather misleading. For example, she referred to Mr. Lim Yew Hock as a totally unknown politician, who was forced by circumstances to assume the position of Chief Minister of Singapore.[67]

We were able to correct any misconception Miss Turnbull consciously or unconsciously tried to tell about the Federation of Malaya.

Vancouver is a beautiful city, but unfortunately we had no time to go sight-seeing. The atmosphere is very English and there is a large British investment. We saw one type of British investment and that was the investment made by the Guinness family in housing estate. Incidentally, we read in the newspapers of a forth-coming visit of Lennox Boyd, and apparently since Mrs. Lennox Boyd is a Guinness they could possibly be coming to inspect Guinness' investment.

Thursday, August 7, 1958

Attended Security Council meeting, at which the subject of the calling of Special Emergency Session of United Nations Assembly was discussed. The

---

[67] Constance Mary Turnbull was at the time attached to the Department of History at the University of Malaya in Singapore (*University of Columbia Reports* Vol. 4, no. 5, May 1958).

United States scored a tactical victory, because its resolution was tabled earlier than the Russian's, when the Security Council met to discuss the question of the Middle East in July and therefore had priority in voting. The debate which ensued centred on the form of resolution to be tabled at the Special Emergency Session of United Nations Assembly, which every member of the Security Council agreed should be called. The United States of America Representative insisted that the resolution should be centred on the complaints made by Lebanon and Jordan to the Security Council, while the Russians insisted that the subject of aggression by United States of America and United Kingdom and the withdrawal of their troops should be the basis of the resolution. United States of America won. The next question raised was under what procedure should the Special Emergency Session be summoned. It turned out that it could only be done by invoking the "Uniting for Peace Resolution". The Soviet was against mentioning this in the resolution to be tabled at the United Nations Session, on the ground that the Soviet never accepted the "Uniting for Peace Resolution".[68] This attitude is typical of the Soviet, who never accepts majority view in any resolutions passed by the Assembly, and it is this attitude also which frustrates the Assembly on many an occasion. The United States of America Delegation compromised by quoting only a reference to the "Uniting for Peace Resolution" to be included while at the same time emphasising that it by no means lessened the embarrassment of the Soviet.

It was therefore unanimously agreed to summon the Special Session of the Assembly.

Friday, August 8, 1958

The United Nations Assembly was summoned at 5 p.m.. Sir Leslie Munro, the President of the Assembly, made a speech in which he implored the

---

[68] United Nations General Assembly Resolution 377 — also known as the "Uniting for Peace Resolution" — was passed in 1950. This resolution was initiated by the USA to circumvent Soviet Union vetoes in relation to the Korean War. When the lack of unanimity in the Security Council causes the body to fail in its duty to maintain international peace, the matter would immediately be debated by the General Assembly to reach an agreement on appropriate recommendations.

Assembly not to engage in recriminations and polemics, but to be restrained in their utterances in the debate.

The Secretary-General in his own characteristic way outlined the course, which he hoped the debate would follow. As it turned out, this was what exactly happened.

The Credentials Committee was appointed having the same composition as the one at the 12th Session of the Assembly.

The meeting was adjourned at 5.30 p.m..

Thursday, August 14, 1958 — Thursday, August 21, 1958

Except for week-ends, the Minister and I regularly attended the Special Emergency Session of United Nations Assembly. Our work was rendered somewhat easier because of the guidance which I received from the Prime Minister conveyed in a Personal Letter.

Our UN Office in New York was working at high pressure. Miss Khoo, our Cypher Clerk, had to work long hours and often late into the night. Sopiee was tireless and energy itself. It was lucky that Sopiee and not Tunku Ja'afar was in New York. Our work would have been much easier, and a lot of time saved, if only we had typex machines.[69]

In view of the importance of the debate and its repercussions in the Federation of Malaya, we decided to take an active part in the debate. To this end Sopiee was entrusted the task of drafting a resolution and "hawking" it around for support, while Ismail and I discussed the type of speech, which would make its mark in the Assembly, and, what was more important, which would help the Alliance Government politically in the Federation. Ismail, by virtue of the ease and the expert manner with which he always wields a pen, was the ideal man to draft the speech.

Although Sopiee was not successful in getting sponsors for our resolution, he did succeed in getting our ideas discussed and finally, partly

---

[69] The *typex* was a cipher machine that had been used by the British, and by Commonwealth countries, since 1937.

incorporated in the resolution, which was accepted by the Assembly, Our attempt to sponsor a resolution soon became well known in the lobbies of UN and I think the publicity thus engendered enhanced the prestige of our Delegation. Unfortunate, the Press unwittingly gave the credit to the Indonesians, who, as far as I know, did not try to sponsor a resolution. To be fair to the Indonesians, it must be admitted that members of their delegation did tell Sopiee that they were getting credit, which was not theirs. It is only right that I should here acknowledge the very creditable work done by Sopiee.

Our speech was well received even by the delegates from the Communist countries, who, although they did not like the specific reference to Communism, thought the speech was fair and unbiased.[70] Subsequently, when we received congratulations from the Prime Minister, we were extremely pleased. I am the first to admit that credit goes to all members of our Delegation, because our achievement was made possible by good team work.

Some interesting comments of the Session are worth recording.

At a cocktail party, given by Mr. Cabot Lodge in his apartment at Waldorf Towers, the Foreign Minister of Canada, Mr. Sydney Smith, approached me and said he would like to show me a copy of a resolution, which Canada was going to sponsor. I did not see the resolution until it was tabled by the seven powers.

Some members of the Arab delegations were shown our draft resolution by Sopiee and they vehemently denounced it, because, they said, its substance was essentially American. And yet, in the final resolution sponsored by all the Arab countries, the substance was very much like ours and the language was definitely milder.

One day, I was walking in the lobby with the Permanent Representative of Sudan, when Dr. Malik, the Foreign Minister of Lebanon, approached and talked to the Sudanese and ignored me. Later, after the final meeting of Afro-Asian at which the final resolution was endorsed by the Group, Sopiee went up to Dr. Malik in order to congratulate him. Instead of responding, he

---

[70] An error in dating occurs here. The speech was made at the UN on 26th September 1958, and not in August, as suggested here. See Appendix 4.

shook his head and walked away. These two incidents were either a deliberate snub or unintentional due to absentmindedness. If the former, it must be due to the fact that our Delegation has not definitely given our word to support his candidature as President of UN at the forthcoming session.[71] If this be the case, then Dr. Malik must be a very unreasonable man to expect our Delegation to give him our word at a time when he was the centre of controversy. I have asked Sopiee to find out the truth.

---

[71] Charles Malik had failed in 1957 to become president of the 12th Session, but did succeed for the 13th Session (See *United Nations General Assembly Official Records*, 678th meeting at the 12th Session, p. 4. New York. See Appendix 4 on Ismail's contribution at the 761st Plenary Session of the 13th Session, presided over by Charles Malik).

EPILOGUE

In a "strictly personal" letter to Tunku Abdul Rahman Putra written in September 1958, Dr Ismail reminded the Prime Minister that it was now time to review "our agreement", which was that he would be stationed in the USA only for a year (Letters). The conscientious person that he was, Dr Ismail wished to have exact clarifications regarding qualifications for electoral candidates. He was worried that Malayans who were not resident in the country during the six months preceding the elections might not be eligible to run for office. He was eager to remain the representative for his old constituency of Johore Timor.

The best time for him to return to Malaya was January or February 1959, since he expected elections to be held in July or August. To play it safe where constitutional rules were concerned, he wished to be resident in the country at least six months before elections — the country's first as an independent state — were held. Furthermore, the General Assembly at the United Nations would end in the middle of December, and if he left immediately after that, there would be ample time for the Tunku to find a replacement for him. He ventured to advise the Prime Minister on the matter of his successor.

> It is superfluous to tell you that practically all countries like Australia, Burma and Pakistan send men who have been Cabinet Ministers to fill these posts. One qualification is very essential. A person must be very loyal to the party in power and must be trusted to carry fully the policy of the government, and not variations of that policy. It is so easy if the government

knowing about it until too late to repair the damage. I think it is preferable at this stage of the history of our country to have a Malay as our Ambassador to Washington and Permanent Representative to the UN. It is for this reason that, as you know I fought tooth and nail for adequate cost of living [allowance] and thanks to you and the other Ministers of the Cabinet the recently approved cost of living is sufficient for a person without private means to be our country's Ambassador to Washington (Letters).

On September 10, he again wrote to the Tunku to advise him not to allow too much time to elapse between his departure from Washington and the arrival of the Tunku's new appointee as ambassador.

Deputy Premier Razak wrote to Dr Ismail on 19 November. He had just secured a huge loan from the Sultan of Brunei at a low interest, "in order to implement some of the short-term projects for the rural areas before the elections". The government was still at a loss as to whom to appoint to replace Dr Ismail. Razak further wrote:

The political atmosphere is getting warmer with the approach of the elections next year, but our stock is higher than it has ever been since independence. As far as the UMNO is concerned the support of the rural people is still solidly with us. However I am not so sure with the MCA. The MCA is not getting the Chinese support in the town and the new leaders of the MCA are trying to rush things a bit with the result that they are losing the support of the good Malayan Chinese. There is now a big controversy over the new constitution of the MCA. [Tan] Siew Sin and Ong Yoke Lin are opposed to the new constitutional changes and [new party leader Dr Lim] Chong Eu is a dilemma. I do not know what the result of all this will be but if the MCA is to get the support of the good Chinese the leaders must come down to earth. As I advised Dr Lim Chong Eu we should not cast the net too wide but should close the ranks. No political leader in this country can expect to get the support of all members of every race but we must always stick to principles and known policies. So long as we are sincere and play a straight game we should be alright (Letters).

Dr Ismail had been very concerned that the Tunku was planning to make Ismail Ali *charge d'affaires* in Washington instead of appointing a new Ambassador. But a letter from the Tunku written on 24 November 1958 put him at ease. The Prime Minister had managed to persuade Nik Kamil, Malaya's High Commissioner to London, to become the ambassador to America instead after he received the assurance that it would not be too long a posting.

> When you return I will pass over to you the portfolio of the Ministry of External Affairs as well as some of the subjects now in Suleiman's portfolio. Suleiman is a very sick man but he is most conscientious about his work, but I feel that unless he can be relieved of some of the onerous burdens, his health would suffer (Letters).[1]

The Tunku warned Dr Ismail that the situation in Indonesia at that time was getting worse by the day, and that his government was being embarrassed by regular visits paid by Sumatran rebels to the peninsula: "However, that would be your headache when you take over my portfolio, and I know you can deal with them appropriately".

As mentioned in the introduction, Dr Ismail's experiences from the United Nations and in the United States formed many of his later ideas on foreign affairs. As External Affairs Minister, as Commerce and Industry Minister, as Internal Security Minister, Home Affairs Minister, Deputy Prime Minister, and also Minister of Trade and Industry, his role in the building of Malaysia cannot be over-exaggerated. He was one of the few first-generation leaders of Malaya who possessed an integrated view on the country's internal problems and foreign affairs considerations.

As was already clear from Malaya's first year at the United Nations, Dr Ismail demanded hard work from his subordinates and colleagues, and would push them almost as much as he pushed himself. His health suffered along the way. Being a medical doctor, he knew his body would not take the punishment and so he retired in 1967. This was for the sake of his young family, he told the Tunku.

Just before his retirement, on 8 June 1966, Dr Ismail became the first to be conferred the newly instituted Order of Chivalry (Darjah Yang Mulia

---

[1] Ismail's elder brother Suleiman was Minister for the Interior and Justice. He was later made High Commissioner to Australia at his own request, but on 7 November 1963 while delivering a speech in Melbourne, he suddenly collapsed and died.

Setia Mahkota Malaysia: The Most Esteemed Order of the Crown of Malaysia). He received the Order's First Class (Seri Setia Mahkota: Grand Commander), after which he was known to the world as "Tun Dr Ismail" (*The Straits Times*, 9 June 1966; Abdullah 1986: 96–101).

After racial riots broke out in May 1969, he returned on Deputy Premier Tun Abdul Razak Hussein's request as Home Affairs Minister, to rebuild the country's parliamentary rule, as it were. He died suddenly of a heart attack at his home at 10pm on the night of 2 August 1973.

Following Malaysia's first state funeral on 3 August, his body was laid out in state at the National Mosque in Kuala Lumpur. The next day, he became the first to be laid to rest in the Heroes Mausoleum on the grounds of the mosque.

APPENDICES

APPENDIX 1

Ismail's inaugural speech during the general debate at the 12th Session

United Nations General Assembly
Twelfth Session
678th Plenary Meeting

Tuesday, 17 September 1957, at 3 p.m.
New York.

President: Sir Leslie MUNRO (New Zealand).

Agenda Item 25 — Admission of New Members to the United Nations: Admission of the Federation of Malaya to Membership in the United Nations.

---

78. Mr. ISMAIL (Federation of Malaya): On behalf of the Government of the Federation of Malaya, I would like to express our gratitude to the President and to the other representatives gathered here for their warm welcome. I would like particularly to express our thanks to the members of the delegation of the United Kingdom and the other Commonwealth countries for the draft resolution which preceded our admission to membership in the United Nations.

79. It is with pride and humility that I speak before you today so soon after the emergence of the Federation of Malaya as an independent and fully

sovereign country on 31 August 1957. I speak here today in this, the greatest assembly of nations, as the representative of a small nation, a nation of only 6 million people, living in an area of only 50,000 square miles. The acceptance by the General Assembly of the membership of the Federation of Malaya in the United Nations confers on my country a privilege and a right which we shall cherish. At the same time, it confers on my country, small though it is, a great responsibility which we envisaged when we set out, with determination and singleness of purpose, on the road to independence.

80. Although our material wealth and our standard of living compare very favourably with those of many nations in the world today, as a small nation, our basic strength lies not in these material things, but in the moral character and purposes of our people. We have in Malaya three major racial groups: the Malays, the Chinese and the Indians, who have lived together for generations in peace and harmony. Neither the difference in religion and cultural background, nor the difference in their economic and social status, has created an insuperable barrier towards the national unity of these races. Our great desire is to have the right and the good fortune to live as a free, independent and united nation among the free nations of the world. The achievement of this desire, through peaceful and constitutional means, through friendly negotiation and a spirit of compromise, is the result of the abiding moral strength inherent in each of the three racial communities living in Malaya today.

81. We suggest that, to a small nation such as ours, as to all small nations, it is in the moral strength of our people that we shall find the inspiration to shoulder the responsibility which membership in the United Nations bestows upon us. Our Prime Minister, Tunku Abdul Rahman Putra, declared, in the Proclamation of Independence for the Federation of Malaya, that the Federation of our eleven States, with God's blessing, shall be forever a sovereign, democratic and independent State founded upon the principle of liberty and justice and ever seeking the welfare and happiness of its people and the maintenance of a just peace among nations.

82. Our King, at the opening of our Parliament, had this to say:

> "It is the intention of my Government to be on the most friendly terms with all countries in the world. My Government stands for peace, freedom and the well-being of every country of the world".

Continuing, His Majesty further said:

> "My Government will adhere to the principles embodied in the Charter of the United Nations and, if the Federation is elected a Member of that Organization, my Government intends that this country should play its part within the bounds which limited resources must dictate in the work of the many international bodies which operate under the auspices of the United Nations".

83. It is now my duty as the representative of the new independent Federation of Malaya, to affirm solemnly in the General Assembly the aim and object of the Government and people of the Federation of Malaya: with the grace of God, to observe the principles and further the purposes of the United Nations Charter.

84. With pride and joy, and an awareness of the grave responsibility before us, we take our place among you today. With God's blessing, we shall not fail in the trust that is placed upon my country and my people.

APPENDIX 2a

Ismail's contribution to the general debate at the 12th Session

United Nations General Assembly
Twelfth Session
686th Plenary Meeting

Wednesday, 24 September 1957, at 3 p.m.
New York.

President: Sir Leslie MUNRO (New Zealand).

---

140. Mr. ISMAIL (Federation of Malaya): Representatives may not be fully aware that the Federation of Malaya has been fighting militant communism in Malaya since 1948 and that my country is the only country in the world today which is involved in a shooting war with adherents of communism. Representatives may not all be aware that almost all the communist terrorists who today are taking up arms against the constituted Government of my country are aliens.

141. We have been fighting militant communism in Malaya for nearly ten years at great cost to the country in men, material and money. Several thousands of peaceful civilians have been killed and injured in this war. We are still spending at the rate of about $100,000 a day in fighting the Communists in the Malayan jungles. These are resources which have to be

diverted to the fight against communist terrorism in Malaya, resources which otherwise could have been used towards the economic and social development of the country.

142. It is true that we are at present getting the better of this fight. My Government, by intensive and careful efforts through every means, has conveyed to the so-called Malayan Communist Party that we are now a fully sovereign and independent country. The so-called Malayan communist party will now be aware that the Federation of Malaya has taken its place as an independent country, as a Member of the United Nations.

143. Surrender terms have been offered to terrorists of the communist party, offering them a chance to live in peaceful pursuits among the great majority of the people, or passage to their countries of origin should they not be able to live in peace and according to democratic principles.

144. We have fought militant communism for many years and this fight has placed, and continues to place, a great strain on our resources. We therefore fully support the recommendation of the General Committee [not to include the question of the representation of China in the United Nations in the debate agenda].

APPENDIX 2b
Ismail's contribution to the general debate at the 12th Session
(...continued)

United Nations General Assembly
Twelfth Session
688th Plenary Meeting

Wednesday, 25 September 1957, at 3 p.m.
New York.

President: Sir Leslie MUNRO (New Zealand).

———————————

75. Mr. ISMAIL (Federation of Malaya): Mr, President, first and foremost I should like to congratulate you on your election as President of the twelfth session of the General Assembly. It will remain in our memory that it was during your Presidency that the Federation of Malaya was admitted to membership in the United Nations.

76. Being a newcomer to this Assembly, I must confess that it was with some hesitation that I decided to participate in this general debate. I should mention right away that as a newly independent nation, fully responsible to itself in both internal and external affairs, the Federation of Malaya is less than one month old. Before 31 August 1957, the external affairs of my country were entirely the responsibility of the United Kingdom Government and we had no hand in them. The people of the Federation of Malaya

assumed complete responsibility over the external affairs of their country as from 31 August 1957, starting, so to speak, almost from scratch. We have been asked right from the dawn of independence what our foreign policies are. We consider that it is appropriate that statements on such policies should be made only in general terms, because it is inevitable that it will take time for us to formulate policies on specific matters, their formulation requiring all the careful study that they deserve. In general terms, therefore, the foreign policy of the Federation of Malaya is to safeguard our independence and to live in piece and harmony with all friendly nations of the world.

77. We are fully conscious of the many and varied problems that face the world today, problems some of which are potentially dangerous to the peace and security of the world and which require solution. We are conscious that as a Member of the United Nations, small though we are as a nation, we have a part to play in the discussion on these vital problems and in the attempt to seek a solution to them. It was not my intention at this stage of our membership of the United Nations to speak on the problems which are before this session of the General Assembly. But after listening to the representatives who have spoken before me, some of whose statements have found a responsive chord in our hearts, I feel that I must make myself heard in this debate.

78. I would like first to express our gratitude to the many representatives for their kind words in this general debate in welcoming my country as a Member of the United Nations. We are particularly encouraged by the statement of the representative of New Zealand [683rd meeting] that the vitality of the United Nations is reflected not only in the scope of the General Assembly's agenda but also in its growing and nearly universal membership. There probably was never a time in the troubled history of the world when so much depended on the success of this Organization to solve those problems which threaten the peace and prosperity of the whole world. The vitality of the United Nations in finding solutions to these problems must depend on its Members, and I have no doubt that the growing and nearly universal membership of the United Nations contributes towards this essential vitality.

79. This leads me to the subject of self-determination on which we have already heard wise words spoken here. I cannot do better than repeat the words of the representative of Ireland:

> "The principle of self-determination of peoples ought…to be the great master principle by which this Assembly should be guided in its quest for a just and peaceful world order" [682nd meeting, para. 291].

80. It is the firm belief in this principle which has brought independence to the people of my country. It was the staunch belief in this principle of self-determination that gave strength to nationalism in Malaya in the fight for independence. We can no longer afford to infringe this principle if we are to seek a just and peaceful world order, We firmly believe that it is the guiding principle which will bring a solution to the problems which have arisen in Africa, in the Middle East and in our own part of the world — problems which the Assembly must face. Colonialism, which is the outright denial of the principle of self-determination, is the root cause of the misery and contention which exist in the world today. It has been the experience of my own country that so long as colonialism existed the energies of the people could not be diverted towards fighting communalism, which was the great bogey raised in the plural society of Malaya, or against militant communism which sought the overthrow of the constituted Government of the country, So long as colonialism existed, the energies of the people subjected to it would always be directed towards its removal and towards nothing else. And this is as it should be. Hard and bitter experience the world over has shown that nations cannot live side by side in peace and harmony so long as colonialism exists in one form or another and the principle of self-determination for all countries is ignored. The domination of territories by colonial powers has led to these colonial territories being used as pawns in the struggle of ideologies in the world. We have a proverb which in my own language states: *Gajah berjuang, rumput juga yang berasa.* When elephants clash, it is the grass that is destroyed.

It is worth pointing out that once a country is freed from the deadening hand of colonialism, once the energies of a colonial people are no longer diverted towards fighting colonialism but are channelled towards their own salvation, history shows that the whole world is thereby benefited. I can readily point to the example of the United States, of Canada, Australia, New Zealand and of course, in our own time, the shining example of India, whose untiring efforts for peace and vast influence in world affairs today we readily acknowledge.

82. Like Ireland, like New Zealand, we are a small nation. Our position as a small, newly independent nation, taking our place in the family of nations, is perhaps unique in the world. Ours is what is known as a plural society in which three major races with different outlooks on life live side by side, and which nationalism has brought close together in brotherhood and unity towards a common goal. Nationalism and our abiding faith in democracy, we believe, will maintain and promote this unity of the races in Malaya, but this time towards the ultimate goals of peace and prosperity for all our people and of friendly relations with all countries. It is obvious to us that the prerequisite to these ultimate objectives is peace. There is not yet a state of peace in my country. As I stated yesterday [686th meeting], we have fought militant and aggressive communism in the Federation of Malaya for the last nine years. Militant and aggressive communism, which has found followers among the alien groups in my country, has taken up arms against the constituted Government of my country and we are determined, more than ever now that we are a fully sovereign and independent nation, to end this useless struggle. Our Prime Minister has declared that it is the aim of his Government to end it by 31 August 1958, the anniversary of our independence.

83. Our position in the world today is unique also in that we are fairly content with what we already possess. We do not seek vast sums of money from our friends to tide us along in our own affairs. We do not covet the goods and chattels nor the territory of others. We have even refused to take the territory of Singapore into our little Federation of States, although the Singapore Government desires its voluntary union with us. We as an undeveloped country of course need assistance in the economic development of the country, particularly in the form of technical assistance. And we have received substantial aid in this form. But the greatest need of my country today is peace and the goodwill of all other countries with which it is our

desire to live in friendship and mutual understanding. We venture to suggest that our unique position permits us to play an impartial role in the affairs of the world. It appears to us that there is need for objectivity in our judgements and actions as Members of this great Organization.

84. We therefore take our place among you with great hopes and faith in the ultimate goodness of mankind. We take our place here in this Assembly with a prayer in our hearts that we shall be guided in our discussions and our decisions by objective considerations. We suggest that we have taken our place in this Assembly as a right properly earned; we feel that the Members of this Assembly have accepted us among them purely on the merits of our position. Now that we are here as a Member of the United Nations, we would welcome all other countries which have earned the right to be a Member of the United Nations as my own country has done, and has so achieved that right.

APPENDIX 3

Malaya's *aide memoire* handed over to the American Secretary of State John Foster Dulles by Dr Ismail on 26 May 1958

Mr. Secretary,

The Government of the Federation of Malaya is submitting an urgent application for loans from the Government of the United States of America because of a financial crisis which threatens the continuation of its Development Plan. As you are aware my Government campaign against the Communists is fought on two fronts — the economic and the military. My Government's weapon against the Communists on the economic front is the Development Plan. It is because of this fact and the fact that Communist success in Malaya will have wide repercussions on the international plane that I have sought this interview, in the course of which I hope I shall be able to emphasise the political aspect of the request for the loan. Before doing so, I would like to thank you for granting me this interview, which I know takes a lot of your valuable time.

The Communists in Malaya had known for some time that their tactic of attempting to overthrow the Government by the force of arms had failed. They are now resorting to a new tactic; that of pinning down the Government to the present level of expenditure on the Emergency, which is running at the current rate of M$126 million annually, so that it cannot continue to implement its Development Plan. Thus far, my Government has succeeded in thwarting the Communists. Now, however, my Government is facing a financial crisis. Without the help of your Government, it looks as if the Communists are going to succeed after all with their new tactic. The Government of the United Kingdom has made it clear that it cannot contemplate giving any further help in addition to the valuable financial help it has already given, and that even where public loans are concerned, the Federation Government cannot expect to raise a loan in the London Market in the near future. With elections only a year ahead and if it becomes clear, as it certainly will, that the cost of fighting the Emergency is a major factor preventing the Government from carrying out its Development Plan, then there certainly will be pressure for recognition of the Communist Party, which is all what the Communists say they want, as a condition for giving up the fight. Further, the Soviet Union, in anticipation of Government difficulties, is not slow to put its fingers on the political pulse of the country, for at the last Conference of E.CA.F.E at Kuala Lumpur, The Soviet Delegation made feelers of offer of financial help, which was promptly turned down by my Prime Minister. Without the aid of the Government of the United States to rescue the Development Plan, the present Government cannot be certain that it will be returned to power with an effective majority in Parliament at the 1959 elections. You are well aware, sir, that the present Government is firmly anti-Communist, is establishing democratic institutions in Malaya on a firm basis, and the only Government capable of defeating Communism in Malaya as an effective political force. Its leaders are dedicated men. In their belief in democracy and democratic process, they know they cannot cling to power forever, but they have hopes that before they went out of office, Communism would be defeated, and the country's economy put on a firm basis, capable of withstanding Communist subversion. Help by the United States Government at this crucial time in the history of Malaya is urgent and imperative.

Such help, if I may add, if given, is once and for all. This is based on the following considerations:

1. The Communists in the jungles are all but beaten. If the present Government's policy of attacking on two fronts — the economic and the military — is pressed forward, the Emergency as such will end, at the latest in two years time.
2. Further increases in taxation will then be possible and the Government will be prepared to raise them if necessary.

3. The establishment of a Central Bank will facilitate the expansion of the floating debt on a sound basis and assist the government in its long term operations.

The economic schemes in the Development Plan for Rubber Replanting, Land Development, Industrial Development, Drainage and Irrigation Schemes, Agriculture and Fisheries, and improvements in the facilities for transport and communications will begin to yield results by way of increased national output, income and revenue.

Finally, in view of the urgency of its financial position, the Government of the Federation of Malaya would greatly appreciate an early reply from the Government of the United States to its request. This urgency arises from the fact that the Estimates of Expenditure for the Ordinary Budget for 1959 are already in the preliminary stages of preparation, and the Estimates for the 1959 Capital Expenditure will have to be put in hand within 4 months. If some assurance of help is not forthcoming within a few months, the Federation Government will have no choice but to cut its 1959 Budget drastically.

APPENDIX 4
Ismail's contribution to the general debate at the 13th Session

United Nations General Assembly
Thirteenth Session

761st Plenary Meeting
Friday, 26 September 1958, at 3 p.m.
New York.

President: Mr. Charles MALIK (Lebanon).
General debate (continued)

———————————

Mr. ISMAIL (Federation of Malaya): This is the second occasion on which we have been privileged to participate in a regular session of the General Assembly since the Federation of Malaya attained its independence on 31 August 1957, and I should like to take this opportunity to reaffirm the determination of the Government and people of the Federation of Malaya to observe the principles and further the purposes of the United Nations and renew our pledge to uphold the Charter.

2. Since the emergence of the Federation of Malaya as a sovereign, democratic and independent State, the intention of our Government has been to be on the most friendly terms with all countries in the world. As is inscribed in our Proclamation of Independence, our State is "founded on the principles of

liberty and justice, and ever seeking the welfare and happiness of its people and the maintenance of a just peace among all nations". In keeping with this, the Government of the Federation of Malaya stands for peace, freedom and the well-being of every country in the world.

3. The Government and people of Malaya have great faith in the United Nations. Our foreign policy is based on this faith in the United Nations and on respect for its purposes and principles. It is our policy to support the Organization. We take every important declaration and decision of the United Nations in earnest. I believe that in this matter we share the attitude and feelings of other small nations, which depend for the maintenance of their territorial integrity and sovereignty and for the fulfilment of their desires for peace, justice and freedom on the willingness of the great Powers to respond to the moral force of the declarations and decisions of this world Organization.

4. The picture of the influence of the Organization in support of the goals of the Charter, given in the introduction to the annual report of the Secretary-General on the work of the Organization [A/3844/Add.11], is most reassuring to the Government and people of Malaya. As has been noted by our esteemed Secretary-General, it is the quiet and unassuming long-term work of the Organization that merits the greatest praise, particularly from those small nations which perhaps derive the greatest benefit from such long-range developments. The increasing degree of economic, humanitarian and scientific co-operation taking place under the aegis of the Organization is, indeed, proof of the quiet fulfilment of many of the purposes of the Charter at the grass-roots level of human endeavour. Although such co-operation rarely elicits sensational recognition, such as is bestowed upon more purely political issues, nevertheless we all recognize the full value and import of these developments and welcome the measured statement of these achievements contained in the Secretary-General's annual report [A/3844].

5. The happy result of the efforts of the third emergency special session of the General Assembly is an example of the willingness of the smaller nations to settle their differences within the framework of the United Nations.

6. As a new Member, with such faith in the United Nations, we have been greatly disturbed by the failure of some of the greater Powers to respond to world opinion as expressed in this great assembly of nations. In spite of the friendly relations so happily existing between our Government and the Government of France, we have been compelled by our abiding faith in the United Nations to join with twenty-three other Asian-African nations in co-sponsoring the inscription of an item on the question of Algeria on the agenda of the present session of the General Assembly [A/3853]. It is regrettable that the Government of France should continue to ignore the resolution which was adopted by the General Assembly at its twelfth session [resolution 1184 (XII)] without any vote being cast against it. We join the other nations of Asia and Africa, indeed of other regions as well, in expressing concern that no steps have been taken by the French Government with a view to arriving at a solution in conformity with that resolution. The French Government has not accepted the good offices proffered by the Governments of Morocco and Tunisia in accordance with the spirit of the General Assembly's resolution. Nor have *pourparlers*[2] in accordance with the resolution been initiated.

7. It is the fervent hope of the Government and people of the Federation of Malaya that the war in Algeria may be terminated as soon as possible, so that peace may be restored in North Africa and the people of the area given the opportunity to channel their energies and resources into the constructive efforts of nation-building, economic development and social and cultural progress. It is our firm conviction that the people of Algeria have a right to freedom and independence.

8. It is also with regret that we have had to join with other Members from Asia and Africa, Western Europe and Latin America in inscribing an item on the agenda of the present session [A/3872] concerning the policies of a fellow member of the Commonwealth — that is, on the question of race conflict in South Africa resulting from the policies of apartheid of the Government of

---

[2] = negotiations.

the Union of South Africa. This question has been before the Assembly since 1952. Year after year the General Assembly has called upon the Government of the Union of South Africa to reconsider its position and revise its policies in the light of obligations under the Charter. These appeals from the vast majority of Members of the United Nations, representing the greater part of humanity, have gone unheeded by the Government of the Union of South Africa. We are taking this stand only because of our determination to uphold the Charter, which calls for respect for human rights and fundamental freedoms for all without distinction of race. We must uphold the dignity and worth of the human person.

9. In expressing our concern at the attitude of a friendly Government which is a fellow member of the Commonwealth, we would at the same time like to take this opportunity to make our position clear on the question of Hungary. We note with great concern the recent events in that country. We gave our support to the inclusion in the agenda of the present session of the item, "The situation in Hungary", which was proposed by Australia [A/3875 and Add.11]. The continued defiance of the resolutions of the General Assembly on the part of the Soviet Union and the present authorities in Hungary and their refusal to co-operate with bodies set up, and persons appointed, by the General Assembly greatly impair the efficacy of the United Nations for the purposes which we are solemnly pledged to further. Our firm belief in the principle of self-determination and in fundamental rights is not confined to Asia and Africa but extends to all areas of the world.

10. The upsurge of nationalism in the Arab world is a matter of which we have become fully aware today. We must realize now that Arab nationalism can no longer be contained, whether by internal or external forces. The rest of the world must allow it to find its own expression and to reach its own goals in its unimpeded way. At the third emergency special session of the General Assembly, all the Arab States demonstrated their capability to find an agreed formula to solve the differences that exist within the same family, the Arab nation. It is our belief that, left to themselves, without outside interference, the States of the great Arab nation will, through deeds, give reality to the words of their joint resolution which all of us so enthusiastically

and unanimously supported [resolution 1237 (ES-111)], thus further promoting the orderly political, economic and social progress which we all wish for the whole Arab nation.

11. In the Arab world, as well as in the other underdeveloped countries of Asia and Africa, there is a growing desire for political progress to be matched by equally rapid economic development which could lead to the social uplift of the masses. The United Nations, through the Economic and Social Council and the various specialized agencies, has done excellent work in assisting economic development in these countries; but more needs to be done. However, as a general principle, we hold the view that assistance from outside, in whatever form, must only be given in order to reinforce and sustain the constructive character of nationalism in these countries. It cannot supplant it in any way, however subtle.

12. Much has been said in this Assembly, as well as outside it, of the desire of well-developed, industrialized countries, especially the great Powers, to assist under-developed countries to improve their economic status. Many and varied are the proposals made but, on analysis, they all have one thing in common: that is, that the under-developed countries must show what they themselves can do, and that they desire to be helped. Against this background, the Government of the Federation of Malaya finds it impossible to reconcile what is professed by well-developed countries, especially the great Powers, with what they actually practice.

13. As is well know, the International Tin Agreement was designed to balance supply and demand of tin so as to hold the price of tin within a range between the floor price of £730 a ton to a ceiling price of £890 a ton. It was agreed by both consumers and producers of tin that this price range was fair. It was fair to the producers because, by guaranteeing a fair price for their produce, they could plan with more certainty not only the future of the tin industry, but also their economic planning as a whole. It was fair to the consumers because the existence of a buffer stock would ensure constant supply of tin for their factories, and the presence of a stable price range would make costs more constant and consistent.

14. The International Tin Agreement is one form of price stabilization which has always been advocated as one solution to help under-developed countries to better their economic status. That Agreement is a good manifestation of the effort made by under-developed countries to help themselves because the initiative for its introduction was taken by them, and my country, as one of the great producers, played a prominent part. And yet, hardly had the Agreement begun to work, when one great Power, the Soviet Union, began to wreck it. By dumping tin on the market the Soviet Union did two things. First, it sold its tin at a price which it would not have dreamt of getting if the buffer stock had not supported the price of tin. In other words, the Soviet Union, a great Power, was selling tin at a price subsidized by the under-developed countries. Secondly, it broke the floor price, because its consistent dumping exhausted the financial resources of the buffer stock manager and thus defeated the objective of the International Tin Agreement.

15. The international tin restrictions have necessitated the closing of mines in the producing countries, with concomitant unemployment. The breach in the floor price as a result of the Russian dumping of tin on the market would further aggravate the situation. More mines will have to be closed and the number of workers losing their employment will increase.

16. I suggest that the Soviet Union should alleviate the harm done to the under-developed countries which have been affected by calling a halt to its present destructive manoeuvres on the tin market, or, better still, by buying back those tons of tin which it has unloaded — thereby proving its regret by deeds and making itself worthy of being called the great Power that it actually is.

17. It is the view of my delegation that international peace and security can be maintained only under conditions of economic stability and healthy growth. It is further the view of my delegation that the more developed Members of the Organization, particularly the advanced industrial countries which are the principal importers of primary commodities, have a duty to participate closely in international efforts at long-term stabilization of primary commodity prices. Such a participation would be in the mutual interests of

both producer and consumer countries, and would contribute in great measure to the reduction of the unfortunate economic imbalance which has characterized post-war world economic growth and international trade.

18. However, it must be firmly pointed out that many, if not all, of the less developed countries prefer to participate in fair trade rather than to depend upon economic aid. Thus, to take advantage of a current drop in primary commodity prices, which results from the unusually large amounts of primary commodities that have been off-loaded onto the world market, without giving serious consideration to the disastrous economic, human and indeed political effects such tactics would have on producer countries, is actually to contribute in no small measure towards the creation of conditions of political and social instability in the world which, in turn, would ultimately lead to the paying of a greater price in seeking a solution.

19. It is our earnest hope that through economic cooperation between the more industrialized countries and the economically under-developed ones, through pooling of our resources in human and material terms, and through the application of modern scientific and technical knowledge and know-how, we shall be able to usher in a new era of economic prosperity and stability, thus laying the foundation for an enduring world peace.

BIBLIOGRAPHY

Primary Sources
- *The Tun Dr Ismail Abdul Rahman Papers, marked IAR at ISEAS Library, Singapore*

Notes   — *Notes by the Ambassador.* 30 December 1957 – 26 August 1958. (Folio 5).

Drifting — *Drifting into Politics.* Unpublished memoirs, Chapters 1 to 16. (Folio 12a).

Letters — *Letters 10 Feb 1938 – 3 Mar 1946.* (Folio 3/1);
       — *Letters 3 Mar 1946 – 15 May 1969.* (Folio 3/2);
       — *Letters and Speeches from 16 May 1969.* (Folio 3/3)

Interview with Tan Sri Zakaria Ali, former Ambassador to the United Nations, and Canada, on 12 April 2006 at his residence in Petaling Jaya.

Interview with Tan Sri Lim Taik Choon, first secretary to Ismail in 1957 at the Malaysian Embassy in New York, and former ambassador to Japan and Australia, on 13 May 2006 at the Petaling Jaya Hilton.

Secondary Sources

Abdullah Ali, Datuk, 1986/2002: *Malaysian Protocol. Correct Forms of Address.* Singapore & Kuala Lumpur: Times Books International.

Andaya, Barbara Watson & Leonard Y. Andaya 1982: *A History of Malaysia.* Macmillan Asian Histories Series. Basingstoke & London: Macmillan Press.

Chung Choo Ming 2002: "Our Queen's Scholars": http://viweb.freehosting. net/QSchol.htm.

Columbia World of Quotations 1996. Edited by Robert Andrews, Mary Biggs, and Michael Seidel. New York: Columbia University Press.

Deery, Phillip 2002: *Malaya, 1948: Britain's 'Asian Cold War'*. Working paper #3, The Cold War as Global Conflict, International Center for Advanced Studies, New York University: http://www.nyu.edu/gsas/dept/icas/PhillipDeery.pdf.

Heng Pek Koon 1988: *Chinese Politics in Malaysia. A History of the Malaysian Chinese Association*. Singapore, Oxford, New York: Oxford University Press.

Jain, R.K. 1984: *China and Malaysia, 1949–1983*. New Delhi: Radiant Publishers.

Leifer, Michael 1974: *The Foreign Relations of the New States*. Studies of Contemporary Southeast Asia. Longman Australia.

Liow, Joseph Chinyong 2005 (Feb): "Tunku Abdul Rahman and Malaya's Relations with Indonesia, 1957–1960", pp. 87–109. In *Journal of Southeast Asian Studies*, 36(1). National University of Singapore.

Ooi Kee Beng 2006: *The Reluctant Politician: Tun Dr Ismail and His Time*. Singapore: ISEAS Publications.

Saravanamuttu, Johan 1983: *The Dilemma of Independence: Two Decades of Malaysia's Foreign Policy, 1957–1977*. Penang: Penerbit Universiti Sains Malaysia.

Sheppard, Mubin 1995: *Tunku: His Life and Times*. Subang Jaya: Pelanduk.

Sodhy, Pamela 1991: *The US-Malaysian Nexus*. Kuala Lumpur: Institute of Strategic and International Studies.

The Straits Times, 9 June 1966, from the New Straits Times Press (NSTP) archival collection on Tun Dr Ismail Abdul Rahman (consisting of clippings in folders, arranged in chronological order).

Tan Liok Ee 1997: *The Politics of Chinese Education in Malaya, 1945–1961*. Kuala Lumpur, Singapore & New York: Oxford University Press.

The National Security Archive, The George Washington University: http://www.gwu.edu/~nsarchiv/index.html.

UBC Reports Vol. 4 No. 5, May 1958. University of British Columbia, Canada. Http://www.library.ubc.ca/archives/pdfs/ubcreports/UBC_Reports_1958_05_00.pdf.

Ministry of External Affairs (MEA) 1965: *Malaysia's Case in the United Nations Security Council*. Documents reproduced from the official record of the Security Council Proceedings. Kuala Lumpur: Ministry of External Affairs, Malaysia.

Appendices

1.   *United Nations General Assembly Official Records*, 678th meeting at the 12th Session, pp. 6–7. New York.

2a. *United Nations General Assembly Official Records*, 686th meeting at the 12th Session, pp. 124–125. New York.

2b. *United Nations General Assembly Official Records*, 688th meeting at the 12th Session, pp. 143–151. New York.

3. *Tun Dr Ismail Papers; Letters (Attachment to correspondence dated 26 May 1958).*

4. *United Nations General Assembly Official Records*, 761st meeting at the 13th Session, pp. 191–203. New York.

INDEX

United States Information Agency
(USIA), 64
University Teaching Hospital, 24, 81

W
Warburg, 58
Weaver, George, 38, 63
West Irian issue, 1, 26

World Bank, 5, 48, 59, 65, 70
World Health Organisation (WHO),
57, 76, 77
World Mission, 5

Y
Ya'acob, Tunku, 79

www.ingramcontent.com/pod-product-compliance
Lightning Source LLC
Chambersburg PA
CBHW021540260326
41914CB00001B/86